ERICH SEGAL

Erich Segal. Photograph by Greg Gorman.

ERICH SEGAL

A Critical Companion

Linda C. Pelzer

CRITICAL COMPANIONS TO POPULAR CONTEMPORARY WRITERS
Kathleen Gregory Klein, Series Editor

Greenwood Press
Westport, Connecticut • London

Library of Congress Cataloging-in-Publication Data

Pelzer, Linda Claycomb.
    Erich Segal : a critical companion / Linda C. Pelzer.
       p.   cm. — (Critical companions to popular contemporary
  writers, ISSN 1082–4979)
    Includes bibliographical references and index.
    ISBN 0–313–29930–7 (alk. paper)
    1. Segal, Erich, 1937–   —Criticism and interpretation.
  I. Title. II. Series.
  PS3569.E4Z8   1997
  818'.5409—dc21   96–53849

British Library Cataloguing in Publication Data is available.

Library of Congress Catalog Card Number: 96–53849
ISBN: 0–313–29930–7
ISSN: 1082–4979

First published in 1997

Greenwood Press, 88 Post Road West, Westport, CT 06881
An imprint of Greenwood Publishing Group, Inc.

Printed in the United States of America

The paper used in this book complies with the
Permanent Paper Standard issued by the National
Information Standards Organization (Z39.48–1984).

10 9 8 7 6 5 4 3 2 1

To John, who sustains me

Contents

Series Foreword *by Kathleen Gregory Klein*   ix

Acknowledgments   xiii

1. The Professor Who Wrote *Love Story*   1

2. Erich Segal and the Sentimental Tradition   9

3. *Love Story* (1970)   19

4. *Oliver's Story* (1977)   31

5. *Man, Woman and Child* (1980)   45

6. *The Class* (1985)   59

7. *Doctors* (1988)   77

8. *Acts of Faith* (1992)   93

9. *Prizes* (1995)   109

Bibliography   123

Index   129

Series Foreword

The authors who appear in the series Critical Companions to Popular Contemporary Writers are all best-selling writers. They do not only have one successful novel, but a string of them. Fans, critics, and specialist readers eagerly anticipate their next books. For some, high cash advances and breakthrough sales figures are automatic; movie deals often follow. Some writers become household names, recognized by almost everyone.

But novels are read one by one. Each reader chooses to start and, more importantly, to finish a book because of what she or he finds there. The real test of a novel is in the satisfaction its readers experience. This series acknowledges the extraordinary involvement of readers and writers in creating a best-seller.

The authors included in this series were chosen by an advisory board composed of high school English teachers and high school and public librarians. They ranked a list of best-selling writers according to their popularity among different groups of readers. Writers in the top-ranked group who had not received book-length, academic literary analysis (or none in at least the past ten years) were chosen for the series. Because of this selection method, Critical Companions to Popular Contemporary Writers meets a need that is not addressed elsewhere.

The volumes in the series are written by scholars with particular expertise in analyzing popular fiction. These specialists add an academic focus to the popular success that the best-selling writers already enjoy.

The series is designed to appeal to a wide range of readers. The general reading public will find explanations for the appeal of these well-known writers. Fans will find biographical and fictional questions answered. Students will find literary analysis, discussions of fictional genres, carefully organized introductions to new ways of reading the novels, and bibliographies for additional research. Students will also be able to apply what they have learned from this book to their readings of future novels by these best-selling writers.

Each volume begins with a biographical chapter drawing on published information, autobiographies or memoirs, prior interviews, and, in some cases, interviews given especially for this series. A chapter on literary history and genres describes how the author's work fits into a larger literary context. The following chapters analyze the writer's most important, most popular, and most recent novels in detail. Each chapter focuses on a single novel. This approach, suggested by the advisory board as the most useful to student research, allows for an in-depth analysis of the writer's fiction. Close and careful readings with numerous examples show readers exactly how the novels work. These chapters are organized around three central elements: plot development (how the story line moves forward), character development (what the reader knows about the important figures), and theme (the significant ideas of the novel). Chapters may also include sections on generic conventions (how the novel is similar to or different from others in its same category of science fiction, fantasy, thriller, etc.), narrative point of view (who tells the story and how), symbols and literary language, and historical or social context. Each chapter ends with an "alternative reading" of the novel. The volume concludes with a primary and secondary bibliography, including reviews.

The alternative readings are unique to this series. By demonstrating a particular way of reading each novel, they provide a clear example of how a specific perspective can reveal important aspects of the book. In each alternative reading section, one contemporary literary theory—such as feminist criticism, Marxism, new historicism, deconstruction, or Jungian psychological critique—is defined in brief, easily comprehensible language. That definition is then applied to the novel to highlight specific features that might go unnoticed or be understood differently in a more general reading of the novel. Each volume defines two or three specific theories, making them part of the reader's understanding of how diverse meanings may be constructed from a single novel.

Taken collectively, the volumes in the Critical Companions to Popular

Contemporary Writers series provide a wide-ranging investigation of the complexities of current best-selling fiction. By treating these novels seriously as both literary works and publishing successes, the series demonstrates the potential of popular literature in contemporary culture.

Kathleen Gregory Klein
Southern Connecticut State University

Acknowledgments

This book exists because friends and colleagues shared my joys and frustrations and were willing to assist in all sorts of ways. I am especially grateful to Debbie Rickard, Beverly Simpson, and Betsy Nielsen—for listening; to Lou Jeffries, librarian at Wesley College—for research assistance; to Jeff Mask, Associate Professor of Religion and Philosophy at Wesley College—for biblical and theological information; to Melissa Borsic, secretary *extraordinaire*—for expert typing and more, far more. You are friends beyond compare.

To my husband John, however, who sustained body and soul throughout the project, I acknowledge my greatest debt. This book is ours.

ERICH SEGAL

The Professor Who Wrote
Love Story

In the spring of 1955, Erich Segal ran the Boston Marathon for the first time. His goal, as he confessed in his essay "The Limits of Sport," was simply "to cover that immense distance," which he did, in the "unspectacular time" of 3:43 (18). When the college classmate stationed at the finish line to record Segal's "historic achievement" missed the moment (he had forgotten to load the camera with film), Segal was "unperturbed." In the moment of achievement he had "experienced a profound psychic metamorphosis. It no longer seemed important," Segal realized, "to have completed the course. . . . For within a new voice loudly shouted *citius*"—faster (18).

Five years later, Segal stood once again at the starting line of the Boston Marathon. In each of the preceding years, he had improved his record on the 26-mile, 385-yard course, but now he stood ready to achieve the "ultimate"—to break the three-hour mark. His time that year was 2:56. Yet once again his "joy was muted. The inner songs of triumph," Segal recalled, "were drowned out by a cacophony of *citius*." The achievement of his goal had simply released him from one dream to dream another. He may have conquered the marathon, but he had not conquered the "self-ameliorating comparative" (18), the inner drive to be faster, stronger, better, that Segal identifies as characteristic of modern man.

This "self-ameliorating comparative" provides a context for the many sides and achievements of Erich Segal. Scholar, teacher, scriptwriter, novelist, Segal has never been content to accept limits, to define himself narrowly. Versatility may, in fact, be the defining characteristic of the professor who wrote *Love Story*, versatility that has its roots in the desire to do more, to be more, to exceed the standard every time out.

Erich Wolf Segal was born in Brooklyn, New York, on 16 June 1937, the eldest of three sons. His father, an orthodox rabbi, was also a sculptor, artist, and musician of some talent, and to him Segal traces many of his own interests. "It was he," Segal once noted, "who instilled in me the love of learning and who made me take Latin as well as Hebrew" (*Current Biography* 387). To his mother, he dictated the biblical and historical pageants that were his first literary efforts. "Remind them," she once admonished her son before he set out on a publicity tour, "that your mother was taking down your epic plays when you were four, and couldn't write" (Martin B1). In Brooklyn, Segal attended the Crown Heights Yeshiva and, even after the family moved to Manhattan, Midwood High School, where he distinguished himself as a straight-A student. Segal also studied at the Jewish Theological Seminary in Manhattan and spent his summers at the Institut Monnivert in Lausanne, Switzerland.

Segal's recollection of these years is bittersweet. "From the time I was the littlest boy," he recalled, "I wanted to be a writer. . . . But I came from a nice Jewish family. What kind of a job was it being a writer?" (Ephron 152). His father, who "dominated" Segal, "wanted me to be a professional person" (Ephron 152), so Segal, the dutiful son, acquiesced to his wishes, commuting long hours between his various schools. The situation made Segal the "odd man out." As he noted, "It is true that I ended Midwood as president of the school and won the Latin prize, but those were isolated. What kind of social life could I have had? I spent my life on the subway" (Ephron 152).

At the age of sixteen, Segal injured—and nearly lost—his right leg in a canoe accident. When he could finally stand and walk on it a bit, doctors prescribed light running to help develop strength in his atrophied muscles. Their prescription led to a lifelong habit—distance running. Under the supervision of his high school track coach, Segal was eventually able to run without limping, first one and then two miles. In typical fashion, however, he wanted to run farther. Before long he was running ten miles a day; years later this long distance runner regularly competed (as much against himself as against others) in the Boston Marathon. (Segal has since given up running and now swims regularly.)

In 1954 Segal graduated from high school and began studies at Harvard University, a place that figures prominently in many of his novels. He ran varsity track at Harvard and in 1958, with composer Joe Raposo, wrote the annual Hasty Pudding review, that (in)famous lampoon of national and campus celebrities. A serious student who would become a serious scholar, Segal earned his bachelor of arts degree in 1958 and was named class poet and Latin salutatorian, the only time in Harvard's 350–year history that one man earned both honors. The following year, he received his master of arts degree and then began work on his doctorate.

As a resident teaching fellow in classics at Harvard's Dunster House, Segal, according to Lance Morrow, an undergraduate resident of the house at the time, made rather "an implausible academic." Morrow recalled that this personable and enthusiastic fellow, "who ran marathon races as a hobby, sang with the Dunster Dunces, wrote music, lyrics, seemed more likely to wind up . . . tinkling the 'South Wind Waltz' after dinner to successive generations in the junior common room" than imparting the wisdom of ages in the lecture halls (*Current Biography* 388). Yet Segal did, in fact, take his place in those halls. In 1964, upon acceptance of his dissertation, "Roman Holiday Humor: The Plays of Plautus as Festival Comedy," Harvard granted Segal the doctorate in philosophy, and he accepted a position as visiting lecturer in classics at Yale University. He became an assistant professor the following year and rose to the rank of associate professor of classics and comparative literature three years later.

Segal's career as an academic seemed certain. In fact, among his peers he had earned a reputation as a scholar and translator of some note. In addition to scholarly papers published in professional journals, Segal had published his revised dissertation as *Roman Laughter: The Comedy of Plautus* in 1968. The book was considered a scholarly breakthrough, for not only was it the first book on Plautus in English, but it was also the first book to explain what made the Romans laugh. In it, Segal also attempted to reach a broad audience by providing translations that made the book accessible to lay readers. In addition to his study of Plautus, Segal has edited a collection of critical essays on the Greek playwright Euripides and has translated three of Plautus's comedies, earning praise for both his style and his interpretations. He has also edited books on Plato, Caesar Augustus, and Greek tragedy. He was awarded a Guggenheim Fellowship in 1968. In 1970, however, the publication of his first novel, *Love Story*, was to alter his career path and his life.

Even before the publication of *Love Story*, Segal had demonstrated a talent for and love of popular entertainments, as his Hasty Pudding credits evidence. During his years as a graduate student, he had supplemented his meagre fellowship by helping to doctor plays in their Boston previews and had also composed a revue, *Voulez-Vous?*, that ran for five days in Boston, its early closing attributed in part to heavy snows. A musical spoof on the Trojan War, *Sing, Muse!*, which Segal wrote with Harvard classmate Raposo, fared slightly better, running for thirty-nine performances off-Broadway in New York in the 1961–62 season. Although some critics panned it, others found glimmers of promise in the musical. In fact, Richard Rodgers, the composer of such successful Broadway musicals as *Oklahoma!* and *South Pacific*, was so impressed by *Sing, Muse!* that he invited Segal to collaborate with him on *You Can't Get There from Here* (Martin B3). In 1974, Segal, who once classified himself as a "failed musical-comedy playwright" (Dye 323), also wrote the lyrics to *Odyssey*, a musical produced at the Kennedy Center in Washington, D.C., and starring Yul Brynner.

In the late 1960s, Segal began to try his hand at screenwriting and soon found himself collaborating on the script to the Beatles cartoon feature film *Yellow Submarine* (1968). The credit transformed him into something of a celebrity on the Yale campus. As he observed to one interviewer, "I became a figure of awe to the kids here. On football weekends they'd bring their dates around to Ezra St[i]les [the campus house where Segal lived] and reverently point out the window of the study in which I'd written 'Yellow Submarine' " (Minoff 3). Celebrity would soon become notoriety, however, with the phenomenal success of *Love Story*.

A novel that began life as an unsuccessful screenplay, *Love Story* was published on 4 February 1970 to less than enthusiastic reviews by critics but to universal acclaim by readers. Almost immediately it vaulted to the top of the *New York Times Book Review* best-seller list, where it remained for a year. One in five Americans read the tragic tale of star-crossed lovers. It was translated into twenty-three languages, topping the best-seller lists in England, France, Italy, Brazil, Japan, and Germany. In December 1970, the film of *Love Story*, starring Ryan O'Neal and Segal's friend Ali McGraw, was released to equally enthusiastic audiences and box office success. Critics may have declared dead the market for old-fashioned sentimentality, but readers and audiences worldwide were eager to pay for what Pauline Kael, film critic for the *New Yorker*, called a case of "the weepies" (54).

The disjunction between *Love Story*'s critical and popular success was dramatically illustrated when the nominees for the 1971 National Book Award, one of the most prestigious literary prizes in the United States, were announced. A poll of five hundred critics, librarians, and publishing representatives had recommended *Love Story* for nomination, but when five judges on the award's fiction panel threatened to resign if it were not eliminated, the National Book Committee yielded to their demands. William Styron, one of the fiction jurors, justified the decision, noting that "it is a banal book which simply doesn't qualify as literature" (Raymont, "Book Unit" A16). Segal, who was himself serving at the time as an NBA juror in the category of arts and letters, took the high road in the controversy. "I honestly don't think I should be placed on the same page with Saul Bellow and John Updike," he stated, but "it was a moral breach to take me off" (*Current Biography* 388). In 1971, *Mr. Sammler's Planet* may have won critical acclaim and the National Book Award, but *Love Story* captured readers' hearts.

Segal's popular success was not without its consequences, especially to his scholarly credibility. Suddenly the professor who wrote *Love Story* found his students and fellow academics questioning his seriousness of purpose. He may have earned a reputation for his scholarship, but it was his credits for the screenplays of *Yellow Submarine*, *The Games* (1969), *R.P.M.* (1970), and *Jennifer on My Mind* (1971)—and, of course, *Love Story*—about which everyone was talking. Students had previously filled Yale's six-hundred-seat Sterling Law Auditorium three times a week to hear Segal's electrifying lectures on classical civilization. Now they were complaining about his flamboyant style: It lacked sincerity and was nothing more than a star turn. Students living in Ezra Stiles College, where Segal held the post of resident fellow, actually mounted a campaign to have him removed ("Erich Segal's Identity Crisis" 16).

A backlash may have been inevitable, but Segal, who was as enthusiastic about his success as he was about his other interests, including teaching, was unprepared for it. As one of his colleagues noted, "He was amazed by success, a kid with a new toy. It never occurred to him that other people wouldn't want to play with it too" (Darrach 77). Although Segal insisted, "I am what I always was—an academic. . . . It's the most important thing I do" ("Segal the Scholar" 53), the controversy undermined both his confidence and his position at Yale. In an interview published in *The New Journal*, the Yale student magazine, Segal admitted to being "uncomfortable" in the classroom for the first time in his career and confessed to being shaken by "an existential trauma" triggered by the loss of his professional identity ("Erich Segal's Identity Crisis" 16).

Stung by the criticism, Segal temporarily abandoned his popular pursuits to devote himself exclusively to scholarship. He even declined an invitation from Queen Elizabeth to attend a Royal Command Performance of the film *Love Story* in London ("Segal the Scholar" 52–53). "If the price of being a professor is never daring to write another *Love Story*," Segal proclaimed, "I will pay the price" ("Segal the Scholar" 53). By the close of the 1971 academic year, however, Segal had followed the advice of colleagues and agreed to take a leave of absence from his teaching position at Yale. As he later revealed to Wendy Smith of the *Chicago Tribune*, "I came within a year of getting tenure at Yale, but unfortunately in that one year, as was said jokingly to me, although I didn't laugh, 'You published one book too many'" (45).

In subsequent years, Segal would return to the classroom, assuming visiting professorships at the University of Munich (1973), Princeton University (1974–75), and Dartmouth College (1976–77). In 1981, he even returned to Yale, where he held the rank of adjunct professor of classics until 1988 (when he was not on leave to promote or write a book). But his days in academe were essentially over. *Love Story*'s success had simply raised too many doubts about Segal's scholarly commitment. As he told Smith, "They were hostile, they were deprecating, they were implying—and sometimes saying explicitly—that I had vulgarized myself, or that in fact I was always vulgar and had showed my true colors" (45). Today, Segal, who makes his home in London, England, is a fellow of Wolfson College, a large graduate college of Oxford University, and an occasional lecturer at colleges and universities throughout the world. Teaching, however, is no longer his primary vocation.

In the seven years between the publication of *Love Story* in 1970 and its sequel, *Oliver's Story*, Segal divided his time between university classes, his Broadway-Hollywood interests, European writing and lecture projects, and other activities, including service on the National Advisory Council of the Peace Corps. All give evidence of his many interests. Perhaps his most unique assignment was a stint as sportscaster for the American Broadcasting Corporation (ABC) during the 1972, 1976, and 1980 Olympic Games, where the distance runner covered track and field events. During this time, he also began to write occasional commentaries on sports and other contemporary topics for *The New Republic*.

In 1973, Segal published his first and only children's book, *Fairy Tale*. The story focuses on the adventures of Jake Kertuffel of Poop's Peak Mountain, who drives the family's "old-fangled model T–4–2" to the big city to trade it for a new "coupe." There he falls victim to an unscrupulous used car dealer, Happy Humphrey, who convinces Jake to accept a handful of beans for his car. Back home in Poop's Peak, a disgraced Jake plants the beans, which grow into a tree that produces dollar bills. The tale, a retelling of Jack and the Beanstalk, is clever and amusing, but also rather superficial. Moreover, its wordplay is probably too sophisticated for children. So far as reviewers were concerned, the tale was nothing more than an attempt by Segal to cash in on his success (Lee and Ross 46).

During this period, Segal also met his future wife, Karen James, a former children's book editor. In 1975, a year after the blind date on which they first met, the couple married. They have two daughters, Francesca and Miranda. In his dedication to *Prizes*, his 1995 best-seller, Segal proclaims that these three women are "my Prizes."

Since the publication of his first best-seller, Segal has published six other novels, all of which have reached the best-seller lists, and has written the screenplays for three of them, *Love Story* (1970), *Oliver's Story* (1978), and *Man, Woman and Child* (1983). Although the screenplay of *Love Story* did not win the Academy Award for which it was nominated, it did earn Segal a Golden Globe Award from the Hollywood Foreign Press Association in 1971. In addition, Segal's 1985 novel *The Class* was named Premio Bancarella Selezione (best novel of the year) in Italy and was awarded the Prix Deauville at the annual Deauville Film Festival. Previous winners of the prize, awarded annually for the best American book published in France, include Norman Mailer, Elie Wiesel, and Gore Vidal.

Despite his popular success and academic credentials, Segal continues to struggle for critical acceptance, for as Mary S. Dye notes, "he has never completely escaped the stigma of being largely identified as a pop writer" (323). Segal, however, is philosophical about his reputation. In a 1986 interview in *Contemporary Authors*, he confessed, "I have this quixotic dream that some day I'll get a little critical recognition for my novels. No one," he observed, "would nominate me for anything in America, except hack of the month." Segal attributed his critical reception to his popular success, which, he claimed, "poisons the possibility of objective critical appraisal." He also takes heart from the knowledge that many of the world's greatest authors were the popular successes of their own time. "Shakespeare," Segal noted, "was the most popular thing going in the theatre in his time, but he was mercilessly panned by the 'serious' critics. He had to die to become a classic" (Dye 328).

If the price of success is failure, as he argues in a 1976 essay about the

American dream, "Slouching Towards America," then Erich Segal certainly might point to his own career and reputation to prove his case. Nevertheless, the professor who wrote *Love Story* has no regrets. As he admitted in a 1985 *People* magazine interview, "But am I really sorry I wrote *Love Story*? Bull——. I'm overjoyed I did" (Chambers 113). Segal's many fans, one suspects, would certainly agree.

2

Erich Segal and the Sentimental Tradition

In a 1985 essay entitled "Heavy Breathing in Arcadia," Erich Segal compared the popular fiction of Aristotle's day to that of his own to arrive at a remarkable conclusion: "there are striking similarities that link the pop papyrus directly to the modern paperback" (1). In theme and situation, in character and plot, the classics scholar and popular novelist observed, the romantic novel has survived virtually intact throughout the centuries, and the sentimental appeal that had captivated the ancient Greeks continues to give a powerful tug on the heartstrings of contemporary readers.

Although he was describing works by writers as distant in time as Chariton of Aphrodisias and Janet Dailey, Achilles Tatius and Rosemary Rogers, Segal might very well have included his own name among the authors who have found the formula for popular success in the sentimental romance. Such a novel, as Segal explained in his essay, "testifies to the insatiable appetite of their audiences for sentimental tales of Virtue Imperiled" (48) and provides readers with a "pleasing catharsis" (1), or emotional release, at its conclusion. It is *Love Story* writ large, but *Love Story* nonetheless, for no matter the scale of the tale or the details of plot, sentiment and its attendant emotions lie at the heart of an Erich Segal novel.

The modern sentimental novel, which had its beginnings in eighteenth-century England and reached its heyday during the Victorian era, "takes its force," according to Fred Kaplan, "from a keen awareness of the mixed nature of human nature. It is an attempt, among other things, to generate or at least to strengthen the possibility of the triumph of the feelings and the heart over self-serving calculation" (16). Sentimentality, in other words, was opposed to rationality and possessed positive values. Sentimental novelists such as Charles Dickens, Kaplan observes,

> believed that there was an instinctive, irrepressible need for human beings to affirm both in private and in public that they possessed moral sentiments, that these sentiments were innate, that they best expressed themselves through spontaneous feelings, and that sentimentality in life and in art had a moral basis. (3)

For these writers, in other words, emotional sensitivity was the sign of moral sentiment.

By the twentieth century, critics of high culture had begun to devalue the sentimental novel. They equated sentimentality with insincerity, with a conscious effort to evoke emotion for the sheer pleasure of enjoying it, and condemned it for being in bad taste. To the sentimental novel they thus attached pejorative, or negative, values, preferring the irony and philosophical rigors of modern realistic fiction to the "sacred tears" produced by sentimental literature. By the 1960s, the raw realism and sexual explicitness of Philip Roth's *Portnoy's Complaint* were unsettling the literary establishment, and "the market for old-fashioned sentimentality in fiction and motion pictures seemed dead beyond recall" (*Current Biography* 387). Among readers of popular fiction, however, the sentimental novel had never really been displaced. It may have lost some of its moral significance, but it had retained its ability to move readers, as the tremendous success of *Love Story* made clear. In fact, the success of *Love Story* prompted Segal to proclaim, "We're on the threshold of a new romanticism, a sentimental age" (Oberbeck 95).

Although both are essentially products of the eighteenth century, the sentimental novel traditionally differs from the realistic novel in plot, character, and style. In his study of the elements of the sentimental novel, Leo Braudy attributes the differences to the sentimental novel's emphasis on the value of emotion. "In general," Braudy claims, "the sentimental novel opposes intuition to rationality; disjuncture, episode, and effusion to continuity and plot; artlessness and sincerity to art and literary calculation; and emotional to verbal communication" (12). Melodrama, with its plots that sometimes stretch credibility to produce a highly charged emotional effect, is also common to the sentimental novel.

Certainly the novels of Erich Segal do not conform exactly to the traditional elements of the genre—he is, after all, writing in a different century and to readers conditioned to certain expectations about the depiction of topics such as sexuality. In their emotional impact, however, and in elements of plot and characterization, Segal's novels, even his most recent multicharacter sagas, have much in common with the sentimental novel that has captivated readers since the time of the Greeks.

PLOT

Sentimental novels typically depend for their effects on the situation of virtue in distress. In other words, characters who exemplify goodness and truth find themselves beset by forces that threaten their lives and happiness. Typically, a romance is the focus of plot development, since impediments to true love undermine the very foundation of the human community, and the novel's conflict is resolved in a happy ending or an ending that is emotionally satisfying in its optimism. Ambiguities are resolved in the sentimental novel, creating a sense of closure and conveying a belief in order and system. In the end, the good and moral heart prevails.

With slight modifications, Segal's novels do indeed rely on the basic plot elements of the sentimental novel. His protagonists, or central characters, may not be threatened by a villain who embodies evil, but their happiness is imperiled by the circumstances of life. Sometimes, as in *Love Story*, catastrophic illness brings an end to the perfect romance. Sometimes, as in *Doctors* or *Acts of Faith*, missed opportunities or twists of fate complicate the protagonist's quest for happiness, success, love. In every case, Segal's characters deserve their desires, so the barriers that stand between their attainment of them seem unjust to readers. Invariably, however, the novel's conflicts are resolved, if not always happily, at least optimistically. Jenny may die in *Love Story*, but her death reunites a father and son. Adam Coopersmith in *Prizes* may not live to collect his Nobel Prize, but the miracle child that his wife Anya carries in her womb at the awards ceremony promises hope for the future. Good and evil may not do battle in a Segal novel, but goodness and happiness are imperiled and readers must confront their own worst fears about the human condition before they experience their release.

CHARACTER

The characters in a sentimental novel tend to be types rather than individual personalities, and to some extent, that is the case with Segal's characters. *Love Story*'s Jenny is the girl from the wrong side of the tracks, and Oliver is its poor little rich boy. In multicharacter sagas such as *The Class* or *Doctors*, Segal takes care to include characters who represent ethnic, racial, or religious groups or embody the experience of women. Segal seldom takes readers into his characters' minds to explore their motivation or emotional lives. Readers know them instead by their words and actions—and by the fact that as stereotypes, their meaning always already exists.

Although many critics fault the writer who uses stereotypes, complaining of their superficiality and incompleteness, stereotypical or representative characters actually play an important role in the sentimental novel. According to Richard M. Gardner, "A stereotype is a simplified concept that is enough understood to guide some actions, but is not analyzed"; for readers, "it brings some emotional (sentimental) overtones" (235). In other words, the stereotypes evoke an emotional response by their very simplicity and familiarity. Full and complex characterization is unnecessary because so much idea and feeling are conveyed by the stereotype itself.

STYLE

Stereotypical characters are also part of the novels' general style, which tends to be elliptical and essentially cinematic. As a writer of screenplays, Segal certainly understands the requirements of the medium and believes that cinematic techniques can be adapted to the novel. Indeed, he believes that they must be. In a lecture he delivered at the Corcoran Gallery in Washington, D.C., in 1971, Segal stated that the novel must become simpler and more direct in an electronic age and that it must rely on dialogue and action to engage its audience (Casey C3). "Let's face it," Segal said at the time of *Love Story*'s publication, "movies are the big thing now, and this is the style that's right for the age of . . . electronic literature. Writing should be shorthand, understated, no wasting time describing things" (Ephron 154).

Commenting on *Love Story*, Mark Spilka offers another explanation for the strategy: "The secret of its popular reception may be found in the sparseness of Segal's style. . . . [He] has left interstices in text and film for his audience to fill, asking them in effect to supply what they already know, to leave out what they fear, and to enjoy what they have always wanted" (796). Cinematic style in a novel demands reader participation and identification, both of which heighten his or her emotional response to the action.

The novels' lack of descriptive specificity is another stylistic element that functions similarly, for as Gardner observes, "A style at least pretending to imprecision tends not to distract from the portrayed experience, and lets us connect flexibility with our own nonverbal experience and ideas" (234). Such is the case for Segal's fiction. Seldom does Segal provide readers with detailed descriptions of his characters' physical presence. The most common adjective used to describe *Doctors'* Laura Castellano, for instance, is "beautiful," a word so vague that readers may easily forget that her blonde coloring defies the expectations of her Spanish ancestry, leaving them free to imagine for themselves the details of her beauty. Nor does Segal individualize his characters' living spaces, their homes, offices, or even their cars. Such spaces often reveal much about their owner's personality and habits of being. Segal's decision not to render them, however, permits readers to fill in the details. This lack of specificity in characterization thus creates the stereotypes that evoke the intuitive knowledge upon which Segal's novels rely for their emotional effect and thematic meaning. As one reviewer noted, "With marvelous economy of words, Mr. Segal conveys feeling rather than mere description, and it is not so much what he does say as what he leaves to the reader to grasp—between the words" ("Coming" 13).

CLASSICAL ELEMENTS

Segal's use of the cathartic ending is another aspect of his fiction worth noting because it connects his work not only to the sentimental novel but also to the classical tradition. As a classics scholar, Segal is certainly familiar with the elements of tragedy: the flawed characters who strive for greatness, the interventions of a cruel fate, the pity and fear evoked by the characters' situations, the release of emotion when their struggle is resolved. While Segal's novels are certainly not examples of classical tragedies, tending more to the melodramatic, they certainly do reproduce some of these elements.

In *Prizes*, for instance, the actions of an omnipotent, almost other-worldly presence, the Boss, shape the life of Adam Coopersmith. Like the most powerful of Greek gods, the Boss summons Adam to his sickbed in the novel's prologue, and the compassionate healer overcomes his scruples about using an experimental treatment to save his life. For the remainder of the novel, the Boss looms in the background of Adam's life, an unacknowledged, unknown force whose presence and power are revealed only in the novel's final chapter. There readers learn that the Boss has been orchestrating Adam's fate, exerting his influence to prevent his former son-in-law from winning the Nobel Prize and then finally relenting to make possible his recognition.

When leukemia kills Jenny Cavilleri in *Love Story*, when *The Class*'s Jason Gilbert risks his life to save the innocent during the raid on Entebbe, when the child of Laura and Barney faces certain death in *Doctors*, readers must confront their own doubts and fears about life. They must acknowledge that even the good and the true are subject to fate and, at times, their own weaknesses. The emotions evoked by such recognitions, however, the pity and fear of classical tragedy, the empathy of the sentimental novel, are ultimately released by the conflict's resolution. Neither life nor death is meaningless in the worlds of Segal's novels, and that fact gives comfort and hope.

SEGAL'S BODY OF WORK

With the publication of his first successful novel, *Love Story*, Segal demonstrated that the market for sentimental romance was not dead. His next two novels, *Oliver's Story* and *Man, Woman and Child*, confirmed the point. All are short tales celebrating old-fashioned love and marriage and values such as honesty, fidelity, and honor. All evoke powerful emotion by threatening their characters' happiness. All rely on summary and stereotypes rather than detailed delineation of character and story to create their effect. Taken together, the three works comprise the first phase of Segal's career as a popular writer.

As the novel's generic title suggests, *Love Story* is formula fiction, a tale of young love opposed first by elders and then by fate and reminding readers of the joy and pain commingling in deep human relationships. In dialogue crisp, clean, and witty, Segal dramatizes the story of Jennifer Cavilleri, a poor Radcliffe student, and Oliver Barrett IV, a wealthy Harvard jock, who meet, fall in love, marry in spite of parental opposition, and then, just as their lives verge on ease and promise, lose one another to death. Marital love, however, is the catalyst to paternal love, as Jenny's death leads Oliver to the meaning of her life and a reconciliation with the father he has hated to love.

The novel was a phenomenal success and led almost inevitably to a sequel, *Oliver's Story*, in which Segal brought closure to the life of his title character. In *Oliver's Story*, a still-grieving Oliver struggles to cope with his loss and to forge a future without Jenny. Neither work nor the promise of new love, however, can entirely fill the void or erase the memory of the woman who taught him to trust his emotions. Nevertheless, life has its own lessons to teach, and by the end of the novel, Oliver has come to terms with his life and his values, and he has acquired a profound awareness of the tragic side of life.

Robert Beckwith, the central character of Segal's third novel, *Man, Woman and Child*, comes to a similar understanding. To do so, however, he must face his own limitations and admit to his own failings when proof of a brief infidelity arrives from France in the shape of a nine-year-old son of whose existence he had been unaware. The revelation of his affair, which Bob had virtually forgotten, nearly destroys his "perfect marriage" and devastates his two daughters, but the strength of the Beckwiths' love and their willingness to grow and change make it possible for them to invite Jean-Claude to be a permanent family member by the end of their summer of discontent.

In 1985, Segal published *The Class*, the first novel of the second phase of his career as a popular writer. A long, multicharacter saga that spans more than a quarter century in the lives of five Harvard classmates, *The Class*, Segal observed in an interview, was "a turning point book for me. It's the first book I've written," he continued, "with a lot of plot, with a large cast of characters, and I really like it. It was an enormous joy to people the world the way [the nineteenth-century French author] Balzac does" (Smith 45). In comparison to the short, sentimental tales that had preceded it, *The Class*, noted Segal, was "a mural," not "a watercolor," and it proved that he could sustain "a big panoramic novel" (Chambers 114).

Like *The Class*, Segal's next three novels are multicharacter stories told against a panoramic background. Together, according to Segal, they comprise "a huge trilogy about men—and women—in white gowns: doctors (*Doctors*), clergymen (*Acts of Faith*), and scientists (*Prizes*)." In these novels of his second phase, Segal follows the personal and professional lives of representative characters to explore the cost of success. Despite their scope, all the novels share certain similarities with Segal's previous sentimental romances: The happiness of essentially good characters with whom readers empathize and sympathize is imperiled by fate and their own personal flaws.

The novels of Segal's second phase are all characterized as well by a solidity of information that is the product of extensive research. For *The Class*, Segal spent years researching Harvard history to give his book the proper backdrop, and *Acts of Faith* involved meticulous research into both Roman Catholic theology and liturgy and Judaism. Segal concludes each of the novels in his trilogy of white-gowned professionals by acknowledging the assistance of experts in the field. To read these novels is thus to learn a lesson about the Unified Field Theory or liberation theology. It is to enter the inner sanctum of the Vatican or to observe the deliberations of the Nobel Prize jury.

THEMES

The development of Segal's body of work demonstrates not only the skill with which he adapts the conventions of the sentimental novel to modern audiences but also the thematic issues and concerns that prompt him to write. A champion of traditional values and virtues, Segal writes sincerely about love and marriage and human commitment. When marriages fall casualty to neglect and human weakness, as they do in *The Class*, *Doctors*, and *Prizes*, a genuine sense of regret surrounds the event. The failure clearly signifies a breakdown in trust, faith, respect, and in countless other values that are crucial to building a human community and sustaining individual integrity. When Oliver rejects Marcie Nash in *Oliver's Story* because she fails to measure up to his standard of right, when Bob and Sheila Beckwith commit to rebuilding their marriage in *Man, Woman and Child*, Segal makes a clear statement in support of virtue, of moral excellence, as a guide through life.

Segal is certainly aware of the temptations and pressures that make it difficult for the individual to live virtuously, as he demonstrates most fully in the novels of his second phase. Chief among them is the desire for success and recognition. Yet the point of these novels is that such rewards are costly. Ted Lambros, for instance, sacrifices his marriage for academic tenure in *The Class*, and the Nobel Prize may not be sufficient recompense for lives half lived. Personal happiness and the fullness of shared love, these novels make clear, are far more valuable than fame and fortune, for neither fills life with meaning, as the experiences of *The Class*'s Danny Rossi and George Keller, *Acts of Faith*'s Daniel Luria, and *Prizes*' Sandy Raven illustrate.

In the end, Segal develops themes that are neither particularly original nor profound. Rather, he taps into deeply held beliefs and ideals that have long sustained his readers. His ability to imbue them with life and thereby uphold their continued value, however, accounts at least in part for the popularity of his novels. With sincerity and conviction, Segal demonstrates his own faith in humankind and in core values shared by all.

3

Love Story
(1970)

What can you say about a twenty-five-year-old Harvard graduate who lost everything?

That his life of privilege was no protection against the force of nature. That adversity tempered his arrogance and love taught him to forgive. That the barrier to his heart's desire was self-imposed. Such is the case of Oliver Barrett IV, the subject of Erich Segal's first novel, *Love Story* (1970).

In this touching tale of love found, love lost, love found, Oliver, an All-Ivy wing on the Harvard hockey team, meets his match in Jennifer Cavilleri, a Radcliffe music major who had set her sights on studying in Paris under Nadia Boulanger, considered by many to be the greatest music teacher of the twentieth century. With nothing in common but love, they marry in adversity, struggle toward success, and then, just as they reach the verge of ease and comfort, a cruel fate bars their admission to the land of promise stretching before them. Jenny's subsequent death, however, is the catalyst that leads Oliver to the meaning of her life, and that understanding results in a tentative reconciliation with the father he has hated to love and loved to hate. *Love Story* is, then, a tale of two loves. To his rather typical story of romantic love, Segal grafts a more compelling tale of filial love that is ultimately the real story of *Love Story*.

Love Story began life as a screenplay, and its path to publication and best-sellerdom was nearly as star-crossed as its lovers' destiny. The characters were based on a young man and woman Segal had known in separate connections. The plot had been inspired by a student conversation that he overheard in 1968. Moved by the tale, he determined to adapt it for the movies. "I sat down and started writing immediately," Segal told Phil Casey of the *Washington Post* in an interview. "The story poured out of me. I changed everything except for the girl's death and the fact that she supported her husband through graduate school" (C3).

Within weeks, the film script was complete, but Segal was unable to find a producer for it. In fact, the scenario was rejected by every motion picture studio in the United States. Acting on the advice of his agent, Segal began to revise the script for publication as a novel, and then his luck changed. Ali McGraw, an old friend whom he knew from her days at Wellesley College, read the script and persuaded executives at Paramount Pictures to film it. Naturally, she would play the role of Jenny. But first Segal would have to make several changes in the story. Jenny, in particular, would now be an Italian-American from Rhode Island rather than a Jewish girl from Brooklyn, as she had originally been conceived (Kanfer 55). When the novel was published by Harper & Row on 4 February 1970, production of the movie, released in December, was already well underway. In both mediums, *Love Story* was an immediate success, soaring to the top of the best-seller lists, where it remained for a year, and scoring at the box office, where it became the most profitable film since *Gone With the Wind* (Darrach 77).

GENERIC CONVENTIONS AS NARRATIVE STRATEGY

Love Story's tremendous success is due at least in part to the conventions of romance and the sentimental tradition on which Segal draws to develop his novel. As its generic title suggests, the conventions of romance, as a literary genre, or type, are keys to the development of both plot and character. In fact, as Richard M. Gardner notes,

> The title predicts that the genre's features—the lovers, their resistance to love, their declaration of love, the first coition [or sexual encounter], their love-talk, their self-giving, the obstacles they face, their moods and attitudes, their feelings, their marriage, their death and tears, and the transcendence of the

superficial into the eternal—will participate in the force that moves toward marriage and death. (239)

These literary conventions have been popularized into the stereotypial plot of star-crossed lovers meant for each other but seemingly doomed never to be joined in love. It is the "boy meets girl, boy loses girl, boy gets girl" tale that gives shape to so many popular novels and films.

Complicating one of these basic conventions—the obstacles they face— is the fact that *Love Story* is also a wrong-side-of-the-tracks romance. It is a contemporary version of John P. Marquand's *The Late George Apley* (1937)—but with a twist. In Segal's novel, the mismatched lovers overturn tradition and marry despite their differences. Jennifer Cavilleri, the novel's working-class, ethnic heroine, is hardly the appropriate choice of bride for the heir to the Barrett name and fortune. Native intelligence rather than family background has been her ticket of admission to the ivy gentility of Harvard-Radcliffe, as Jenny is uncomfortably aware. Her disdain for "preppies" such as Oliver, for instance, is in part a defense against feelings of inferiority, and on the occasion of her introduction to the Barretts, Jenny confesses to Oliver that she wished her name were Wendy WASP (48). Jenny's "negative social status" (56) is a powerful impediment to her union with Oliver, yet it is also a plot device guaranteed to win the reader's sympathies. Such an arbitrary and unfair handicap should never be allowed to triumph over true love.

In *Love Story*, romance conventions function as "trigger features," to borrow a term from Gardner. They "activate what we already know, or think we know, without explanation or tedious detail, but with striking emotional effect" (235). That emotional effect links Segal's novel to the sentimental tradition, to a type of literary work in which the characters' heightened emotional response to events produces a similar response in readers. Working within this tradition, Segal first fashions characters with whom his readers identify and then creates situations that elicit their deepest emotions.

Love Story is unabashedly sentimental. In fact, one reviewer complained that the novel "skips from cliché to cliché with an abandon that would chill even the blood of a True Romance editor" (Oberbeck 95). Segal, however, makes no apologies for this aspect of his novel, perhaps, as a classics scholar, understanding that emotion can be a guide to truth. "We're on the threshold of a new romanticism, a sentimental age," he observed on the publication of *Love Story* (Oberbeck 95). The statement suggests the deliberate intention behind his use of generic conventions and his evocation of powerful emotions.

CHARACTERIZATION

Love Story's genesis as a film script accounts at least in part for the novel's strengths and weaknesses of characterization. Like a screenplay, the novel is written almost entirely in dialogue, and that dialogue moves the narrative briskly to its heart-wrenching conclusion. Crisp, clever, and utterly modern, the exchanges between Oliver and Jenny also ring true, even in their use of profanity, and they are thus made believable as characters.

At their first meeting, for instance, Jenny vouches for her superior intelligence by her refusal to have coffee with Oliver. "Listen—" he retorts, "I wouldn't ask you." "That," Jenny quietly triumphs, "is what makes you stupid" (11). Later, during a study date, Jenny warns Oliver that he is bound to fail if he does nothing but watch her study. Defending himself from the truth, Oliver insists that he is studying, to which Jenny retorts, "Bullshit. You're looking at my legs." "Only once in a while," Oliver confesses, and then goes on attack: "Listen, you narcissistic bitch, you're not *that* great-looking!" Disarmingly agreeable, Jenny then delivers her own verbal punch: "I know. But can I help it if you think so?" (38). Such verbal sparring is entirely appropriate for college students too cool to let down their guard and be forthright about their emotions, and such is indeed the case of Oliver and Jenny early in their relationship. Through dialogue, Segal gives life to his characters. They reveal themselves in every word they speak.

Language serves both Jenny and Oliver as defensive and offensive weapons. It allows them to deflect the criticism and insincerity hurled at them, however unintentionally, by others and to repel any gestures of kindness and concern that could undermine their fierce independence. Armed with wisecracks, they are tough and seemingly invincible. Nothing can penetrate their essential integrity of being. Yet the very fact that they rely upon language for protection exposes the bravado in their attitudes. Neither is as invulnerable, as independent, as he or she appears to be.

Their vulnerabilities, however, especially in Jenny's case, Segal barely probes. This omission results from the novel's dependence on dialogue for character development. Because Segal seldom takes readers into his characters' minds to reveal their unspoken thoughts and feelings, Jenny and Oliver are rather one-dimensional. Except for Oliver, the narrator, they are given little opportunity for growth and change, and even Oliver's transformation at the novel's end lacks to some degree the depth that either authorial commentary or self-analysis would provide. Secondary characters such as Jenny's father and Oliver's parents are even less realized. There are, in fact, little more than stereotypes of the doting, ethnic parent and the distant aristocrats. Thus, the same dialogue that propels the plot and vivifies the major characters, and is thereby one of the novel's strengths, is also one of its weaknesses.

The lack of fully rounded characters results as well from Segal's choice of a first-person narrator for his novel. In using a first-person narrator, Segal also limits the novel's point of view, or the perspective from which the reader sees and understands the characters and events. A first-person, "I," narrator has the advantage of lending a sense of immediacy and authenticity to a novel. The narrator is, after all, witness to or a participant in the action. Because the characters and events are filtered through the mind of the "I," however, the reader's understanding of them is only as good as the narrator's. Personal bias and lack of information can thus render suspect the narrator's vision. Oliver's animosity toward his father, for instance, makes it impossible for the reader to trust his judgment of a man whose actions are hardly those of the heartless ogre his son presents him to be. Use of the first-person narrator also prevents Segal from revealing the minds of the other characters, for unless they choose to confide in Oliver, readers cannot know their thoughts and feelings. The limitations of first-person narration, then, like the limitations of dialogue, account for the sketchlike quality of *Love Story*'s characterizations.

Rendered almost entirely in dialogue, Jennifer Cavilleri, the novel's doomed heroine, is at her death what she was when Oliver met her— an intelligent young woman whose generosity of spirit endears her to family and friends. The only child of an Italian-American baker, Jenny had been raised by her father, Phil, following the death of her mother in an automobile accident, and the two are bound by mutual love and admiration. Father is justifiably proud of his daughter's talents and achievements. So, too, are the neighbors who have watched Jenny's growth with an equal measure of pride and concern, the force of which Oliver is made to feel on his first visit to the Cavilleri home (63). Although she is a lapsed Catholic, Jenny adheres to a firm standard of personal behavior and common human decency, and one of her highest principles is the sanctity of the parent-child relationship, a belief that she has clearly inherited from her father (65). This principle will be the source of the only real conflict between Jenny and Oliver, who is throughout the novel intent on rejecting his own father and all that he represents. Because Jenny is a static character, remaining unchanged by the events of the plot, she serves primarily as a foil, or contrasting character, to Oliver, the novel's protagonist, or central character. The differences between them will eventually highlight Segal's thematic insights.

As the protagonist, Oliver Barrett IV is the most dynamic of the characters. He does indeed grow and change through his relationship with Jenny and in his relationship to his father, however superficial his development may be. Heir to both power and position by virtue of his connection to colonial ancestors, Oliver wears both his fortune and his name like an albatross around his neck. He is embarrassed, for instance, by the fact that many of the buildings on the campus of his alma mater are "colonial monument[s] to [his] family's money, vanity, and flagrant Harvardism" (12). As talented and accomplished as Jenny, he is chosen marshal of his Harvard graduating class and accorded the honor of leading the processional. Later, during law school, he earns a coveted position on the *Harvard Law Review*. Fiercely competitive, Oliver, as he admits, has grown up with the notion that "I always had to be number one" (9), so he is not above playing dirty hockey. His chief competitor in all arenas, however, is his father.

To his son, Oliver Barrett III is known variously as "OB III," "the Sonovabitch," and "Old Stoneyface," names that give every indication of Oliver's disdain for his father. A former Olympic rower and a successful businessman, Mr. Barrett has, by his own achievements, set a high standard of accomplishment for his son, a standard that Oliver both resents and fears (35). On the one hand, Oliver wishes to reject his father's expectations of him, to be, instead, his own person. On the other hand, he doubts his ability to measure up to the Barrett legacy. Oliver conceives of his relationship with his father as competitive in nature, and experience has taught him that he seldom wins. During the meeting at which he fails to secure his father's approval of his marriage to Jenny, for instance, Oliver senses the "enormous satisfaction" his father takes in prevailing on a particular point and thinks, "I could tell he regarded it as another in his many victories over me" (59). Oliver's strained relationship with his father lies at the heart of *Love Story*. It is, in fact, the novel's true thematic focus.

THEMATIC DEVELOPMENT

On the surface, *Love Story* appears to be a tender tale of romantic love. Certainly the novel's romance plot and its use of generic conventions, as previously noted, give that impression. Oliver's love of Jenny leads him to increased self-awareness as well as empathy for others. Oliver, for instance, is surprised to find that lovemaking awakens in him a tenderness of which he has been unaware (39). He also acknowledges Jenny's "ability to see inside" him, which forces him to confront aspects of his own being (56–57). Loving Jenny, in other words, makes Oliver a better person. It develops his capacity to love and thereby reinforces a truism of romantic love.

While delineating the obvious is one of *Love Story*'s thematic issues, it is not its central theme. The source of every real conflict in the novel is the relationship between Oliver and his father. It prompts gentle chiding from Phil, provokes a profound disagreement with Jenny, and creates the palpable tension resonating from so many key scenes. In literature, resolution of conflict is a clear indicator of thematic intent, and so it is in *Love Story*. Jenny's love may teach Oliver to love, but Jenny's death helps Oliver to love his father. In this resolution to the novel's central conflict lies the meaning of *Love Story*.

Oliver is in large part at fault for his strained relationship with his father. Granted, Mr. Barrett is undemonstrative and unduly formal. Granted, he and Oliver do indeed seem to engage in what Oliver thinks of as their "continuing series of nonconversations" (26). Granted, he seems authoritarian and uncompromising. But he does at least make an effort to reach his son. Mr. Barrett, for instance, is one of the few Harvard fans to make the journey to Ithaca, New York, for the decisive game for the Ivy title, and the reason, the reader suspects, is not to watch the hockey game but rather to watch his son. In contrast, Oliver, as Jenny accuses, will "stop at [nothing] just to get to [his] old man" (56). If they engage in nonconversations, it is because Oliver attributes his own hostility to his father and consequently misinterprets his questions and gestures. As he tells Jenny early in their relationship, he and his father are fighting a war (36).

Two scenes illustrate most clearly the mutual failures that separate father from son. The first is a strained dinner following Harvard's loss of the Ivy title game. Over steak and apple pie, Mr. Barrett makes every effort to engage his son in meaningful conversation, asking with concern about the injuries Oliver had sustained in the hockey game and inquiring with interest about the status of his law school application. Oliver's terse responses, one or two words or a brief sentence that barely conceals his mistrust and hostility, effectively close off any avenues of communication. Yet Mr. Barrett presses on to seemingly more neutral territory, asking his son's opinion of the Peace Corps, even in the face of Oliver's biting sarcasm (26–29). So hostile is Oliver to his father that he cannot conceive of any genuine feeling in Mr. Barrett's questions. Moreover, Oliver attributes to him all sorts of ulterior motives, most of which hinge on Oliver's humiliation. So preoccupied with his own hurt and so frustrated by his own sense of failure is Oliver that he cannot conceive that the conversation may not be entirely about him, as the eventual announcement of his father's appointment to head the Peace Corps makes clear (54). For his part in the evening's failure, Mr. Barrett is so reserved that he simply cannot share his triumphant news with his own son, much as his choice of topic reveals his desire to do so. And thus the chasm between father and son widens.

That chasm seems incapable of being bridged, as a second interview between the Oliver Barretts late in the novel suggests. Having severed his relationship with his father when Mr. Barrett withheld approval of his marriage to Jenny, Oliver is forced by Jenny's illness to swallow his pride and seek financial assistance from the man he habitually addresses as ''Sir.'' Their meeting, the first in three years, takes place in Mr. Barrett's office, as if to emphasize the businesslike nature of their formal transaction. Yet despite the cool civility with which they conduct their business, an undercurrent of unresolved passion charges their exchange. Oliver is clearly, but surprisingly, aware that his father wishes to talk, that he is stalling for time and searching for a topic of conversation, yet he can do nothing to ease the situation. Like his father, Oliver is willing to talk, but he does not know how. Separated by pain and pride, both father and son are unable to find the ''mutual'' ground (117) on which to prolong their meeting and break the impasse between them.

Oliver's lack of understanding of the parent-child relationship may account in part for his inability to parent. Certainly his and Jenny's failure to conceive a child functions thematically in the novel. Although Oliver imagines himself a different sort of father to his own son, a two-hundred-forty-pound diapered bruiser named Bozo, than his father was and is to him, his fantasies of parenthood contradict this self-image. Convinced that Bozo will be a great athlete, Oliver rejects Jenny's cautionary admonition that their son may lack coordination or be a scrawny weakling. Should Bozo be small, Oliver will simply "feed him up," and should he refuse to eat the diet supplements that will transform him into his father's "idyllic vision," Oliver will simply force him to comply. "He'll eat, goddammit," Oliver exclaims to Jenny, "getting slightly pissed off already at the kid who would soon be sitting at our table not cooperating with my plans for his athletic triumphs" (100–101). As an imaginary parent, Oliver rules the life of his fantasy son much the same way that he perceives his father to rule his. Oliver's childlessness is thus an appropriate extension of Segal's thematic concerns. A man who understands so little about the nature of the parent-child relationship, who is himself an ungrateful son and who imagines himself a tyrannical father, simply has not earned the right to parenthood.

The relationship between the Barretts, real and imagined, is a stark contrast from that shared by Jenny and Phil Cavilleri. In fact, the Cavilleri parent-child relationship is in literary terms the perfect foil to the Barrett parent-child relationship, and as such, it serves to clarify the novel's thematic focus. For most of Jenny's life, Phil had been both mother and father to his only child, and this modest baker from Cranston, Rhode Island, had done all he could to foster his daughter's talents and to nurture her development of self. Their mutual love and respect ring clear in the teasing banter that father and daughter exchange with each other. It is typified by Phil's complete and unhesitating acceptance of Jenny's announcement that she intends to marry a penniless Oliver Barrett. A simple ethic of parental love supports the Cavilleri relationship. As Phil explains to Oliver, "A father's love is to be cherished and respected. It's rare" (65). It is a view that Jenny shares with her father. In fact, it is Jenny's deep commitment to this ethic that precipitates one of the crises in her marriage, a crisis that focuses on the novel's central theme of parental love.

On the occasion of Mr. Barrett's sixtieth birthday, Jenny attempts to effect a reconciliation between father and son by convincing Oliver to accept the invitation to the celebratory party. Drawing on all her powers of persuasion, she appeals to Oliver's love—of his father, of her, but Oliver is adamant in his refusal to attend. During the telephone conversation that conveys the unhappy news to Mr. Barrett, Jenny, sensing his disappointment and hurt, is reduced to tears and attempts to comfort his pain by offering a message of love from Oliver, a message that her husband has not, in fact, expressed. Enraged by Jenny's interference,

Oliver rips the phone from its socket, hurls is across the room, and curses his wife (86). In an instant, Jenny is gone, and Oliver spends the night in tormented search for her.

Their quarrel is inevitably resolved (in the scene that includes the novel's most famous line of dialogue—"Love means not ever having to say you're sorry") (90). Yet the source of their conflict continues to fester beneath the surface of their life together. But for Oliver to understand truly the lessons of love that Jenny has been teaching, the heroine must be sacrificed. "Jenny's role," as Mark Spilka notes, "is to bring the Barretts together, to make them realize their affection" (789). She "lives and dies," argues Spilka, "in accord with nineteenth-century myths of women as moral and spiritual guides for unworthy men and of young girls as the best and purest of those guides" (796). Jenny's death, therefore, can effect the change in Oliver that will allow him, in the novel's final scene, to grieve in his father's embrace. Only Jenny's death will achieve the parental reconciliation that is the thematic focus of *Love Story*.

The novel's structure also reinforces this focus and Jenny's sacrificial role. Certainly Jenny's death of some unnamed blood disorder is an emotional center of *Love Story*, but that scene is no more moving than the novel's closing encounter between Oliver and his father. When Mr. Barrett appears at the hospital, having known instinctively that only some serious motive would prompt his son to ask for money, Oliver can no longer doubt his father's love or misinterpret his motives. He can no longer reject this man who will not be rejected—nor does he wish to. When Mr. Barrett whispers a "stunned" (123) apology at the news of Jenny's death, Oliver shares with him Jenny's own lesson of love, thereby revealing his understanding and acceptance of real love. Those who share such a bond need not speak it; they simply know it, as Oliver does now, in the arms of his father.

In this final scene, not in that of Jenny's death, lies the real meaning of *Love Story*. Otherwise the scene would be anticlimactic, a disappointing descent from the preceding emotional rise. That it is not makes clear Segal's thematic intent. From the beginning of the novel, when her death is announced in the opening line, Jenny has been little more than a ghostly presence in Oliver's life. Now, in the final scene, her ghost, evoked by her words, binds together two men whose love story has always haunted her own. With the powerful scene of reconciliation, the novel must, and does, end.

A PSYCHOLOGICAL READING OF *LOVE STORY*

As an exploration of the parent-child bond, *Love Story* certainly lends itself to psychological interpretation. Such readings apply the strategies of Freudian, Jungian, or some other theory of human psychology to fiction to explain characters' motivation and action in clinical terms. In *Love Story*, Oliver's inability to express his love for his father may be understood as evidence of an unresolved Oedipus complex.

According to Freud, every child experiences latent sexual feelings toward the parent of the opposite sex. He named these complex feelings after Oedipus, who in fulfillment of an oracle kills his father and marries his mother in the ancient Greek tragedy by Sophocles, *Oedipus Rex*. Freud theorized that these feelings were initially positive, but if they were unresolved, they could be the source of adult personality disorder. In other words, the child must eventually suppress his or her sexual attraction to the parent of the opposite sex and identify with the parent of the same sex to become a fully integrated adult. Failure to achieve this transfer of affection and identity leads inevitably to psychological turmoil in adulthood.

Oliver has clearly moved beyond one stage of development, for he certainly does not harbor conflicted feelings about his mother. Nor is she the cause of his inability to love. In fact, she is largely absent from the novel, appearing only in chapter 7, where she merely performs her social function as appendage to Mr. Barrett. Oliver, however, has no such certainty about his feelings for his father because he misunderstands them. In transferring his affection and identity from his mother to his father, a necessary step to resolve the Oedipal complex, Oliver has confused filial love, which is right and proper, with sexual love, with a homoerotic impulse that society condemns as unnatural. Oliver's confusion thus makes him fear to love his father.

Oliver's fierce competitiveness toward his father is primary evidence of the love-hate nature of their relationship. Mr. Barrett, as Jenny tells Oliver, loves his son: "He loves you just the way you'll love Bozo" (84), the child that Oliver expects someday to father. Such love is right and proper. It is, in fact, a natural development of a son's transfer of affection from the mother to the father and of his identification with the parent of the same sex. Yet love for the parent of the opposite sex has contained an element of erotic, or sexual, love that is unacceptable between members of the same sex. Because he fears that this love for his father is unmanly, Oliver disguises the feelings that make him uncomfortable by donning an antagonistic mask. Competition is manly. In the business world, on the athletic field, in the political arena, competition is the accepted means by which men engage in relationships. Competition is thus the means by which Oliver expresses love for his father—only he fails to acknowledge it as such. As Jenny tells Oliver, "You Barretts are so damn proud and competitive, you'll go through life thinking you hate each other" (84).

In his love for his father, Oliver also fears a loss of self. Mr. Barrett has, for Oliver, the power to "make" his son conform to the family tradition. As Oliver tells Jenny, his father makes him do "the right things" (35). He expects his son "to deliver x amount of achievement every single term" (35), and Oliver resents both the expectation and his compliance with it. To maintain some sense of separate self, Oliver sets himself in opposition to his father, rebelling against paternal love and domination. In fact, Oliver's marriage to Jenny, as both she and Mr. Barrett are well aware, is a supreme act of rebellion (56; 58), for a working-class, ethnic girl is hardly the wife the aristocratic Barretts would have wished for their son. Transforming his father into a powerful opponent of self, Oliver, as Spilka notes, "thus protect[s] himself from engulfment and from his own tender feelings" (788).

Ultimately, the lessons of love that Oliver learns from Jenny help to resolve the Oedipal conflicts that threaten to diminish his life. She teaches him that there is nothing unmanly about tenderness, and she provides him with a model of ideal manhood—her own father. Thus Jenny teaches Oliver to love his father, and that is the real love story in *Love Story*.

4

Oliver's Story
(1977)

Perhaps it was inevitable, given the tremendous success of *Love Story*, that Erich Segal would write a sequel to his first novel. After all, that tender tale of heartbreaking love had ended with the death of its heroine. Its hero, Oliver Barrett IV, bereft and grieving, had taken comfort from an unlikely source—his father. Yet the loss of a love like Oliver and Jenny's was not, readers knew, something from which one easily recovered. For Jenny, Oliver had forsaken his family. For Oliver, Jenny had forsaken a chance to study in Paris with Nadia Boulanger, one of the twentieth century's most important music teachers. However would Oliver survive alone?

Yes, it was inevitable that Segal would write a sequel to *Love Story*, and in 1977, that sequel, *Oliver's Story*, rose rapidly on best-seller lists. In it, Segal charts the progress of a still-grieving Oliver toward a tentative resolution of guilt and acceptance of loss that are the necessary prerequisites to life without Jenny and a future of his own. In it, Segal also extends the primary focus of his previous novel, Oliver's relationship with his father, through an examination of the binding ties of family. *Oliver's Story* is, then, a novel that brings closure (or at least a certain amount of it) to the love stories in *Love Story*.

Oliver's Story begins eighteen months after the death of Jennifer Cavilleri Barrett in *Love Story* had burdened Oliver, her husband, with a bad case of survivor guilt and the constant ache of loss. Although he had found some immediate comfort in the arms of his estranged father, neither his love nor his father-in-law's concern and encouragement are sufficient to bring Oliver back into the land of the living. His spirit crushed, Oliver seeks refuge in work and running and even therapy, but nothing helps. And then he runs into Marcie Nash, a woman capable of making him feel again. Oliver will find, however, that the ghosts of the past are not easily vanquished, nor should they be.

CHARACTERIZATION

In his essential nature, the Oliver Barrett of Segal's sequel is merely an extension of the cocky competitor who concealed his insecurities behind a barrage of words in *Love Story*. Grief and loss have not tempered Oliver's character. Rather, they have made him angry and even, perhaps, a bit more insecure. When Oliver, for instance, opens the drawer in which he keeps Jenny's glasses, the only possession of his wife that he has saved, he is reminded "of the lovely eyes that looked through them to look through me" (22) and must invariably wonder how to survive without the woman who so utterly understood him.

The loss of such a woman has made Oliver angry, and he channels his anger into his work. Despite the tentative reconciliation between father and son at the end of *Love Story*, Oliver has not assumed his place in the family textile business. Instead, he champions the rights of the little guy. From the plush offices of a New York law firm, he battles the injustices that he can control, having been cruelly victimized by one that he could not (19). When he isn't venting his anger in the courtroom, Oliver is volunteering his time in Harlem or running. In other words, he is doing anything he can to ease the pain of loss, to escape from the reality of his solitary existence.

Yet escape is clearly impossible, for Oliver lashes his pain with the whip of his guilt. The fact that Jenny is dead and he lives is nearly incomprehensible to him and reason enough to suffer from survivor guilt. But the realization that he had prevented Jenny from living fully the life that was hers is nearly intolerable. To marry Oliver, she had, after all, abandoned her dream of a career in music and had worked instead to advance her husband's education and future. Moreover, his stubborn refusal to reconcile with his family had foisted all the burdens of their short married life on his wife. Now he suffers the consequences of what he judges to be his arrogance and selfishness (50–51).

Like the self of old, Oliver continues to use language as a weapon, but now, following Jenny's death, his cleverness is intended to create a barrier between him and others rather than to impress. Wit keeps his relationships superficial, thus preventing others from penetrating his hard shell of hurt. Against such a weapon, the kindness of Stephen Simpson, Oliver's Harvard classmate, the compassion and intelligence of Joanna Stein, a potential love interest, and even the camaraderie of Phil Cavilleri stand little chance of disarming him.

Even Marcie Nash, the novel's love interest, finds it difficult, and finally impossible, to conquer Oliver. Heir to and director of the Binnendale department store empire, Marcie is everything that Jenny was not. Blonde, athletic, wealthy, and well-connected, Marcie is every bit as competitive as Oliver. In fact, she bests him on the jogging path where they first meet (58–61) and is a formidable opponent on the tennis court, where they play a game of verbal and physical one-upmanship early in their relationship (62–66). Mysterious about her personal life, Marcie intrigues Oliver. A woman whose "single fault was that she didn't have an obvious, convenient fault" (97), she challenges Oliver to live again.

As a character, Marcie is rather one-dimensional. In fact, the superficiality of her characterization is epitomized by a one sentence description: "She was dressed in money" (67). A divorce has made Marcie wary of men, and her competitive drive was born of a need to earn her father's respect and attention (116–17). Segal, however, does not probe these vulnerabilities. Only within the world of this novel is her character clearly defined, for Oliver, not Marcie, is the focus. She is a woman who commands respect for her competence in the business world, and she is not afraid to be assertive.

Marcie's role in the novel is as clearly defined as her character. Her relationship with Oliver will help to heal the pain of Jenny's loss by making him feel again. It will also prompt Oliver to confront the issues that have long prevented him from achieving a strong sense of self. As he struggles to build a relationship with Marcie, Oliver will instead resolve a relationship central to his very being—his relationship with his father. Marcie and Oliver's relationship is, then, crucial to the thematic development of *Oliver's Story*.

NARRATIVE STRATEGIES: METAPHORICAL PATTERNS AND THE CONFIDANT

Metaphorical Patterns

In developing his characters, Segal relies on two metaphorical patterns, both of which convey some essential truth about Oliver, Marcie, or their relationship. One pattern associates Oliver with ill health by linking him to a series of physicians and by using medical language to describe his emotional state. Another pattern uses places of residence to embody their occupants' essential natures. These metaphors, or implied comparisons, provide some indication of Segal's development as a writer, for such self-conscious literary devices are virtually absent from *Love Story*.

That Oliver is suffering is one of the self-evident truths of his story. That his suffering is a sign of ill mental health, however, Segal conveys through the use of a medical metaphor. Language is one of the vehicles that carries the weight of the metaphor. The novel's first line, for instance, "Oliver, you're sick" (11), announces the "startling diagnosis" of an unlikely medical practitioner, Phil Cavilleri, and his patient will confess that after the "Novocaine of [Jenny's funeral] ceremony" (16) had worn off, he consulted his father-in-law to learn "what remedy he might suggest that could be balm for me" (17). Although others see his move into a new apartment as a sign "pointing to my imminent recovery" (22), Oliver knows that only "surgery: Incisions in the soul" (52) will cure his heartsickness.

The preponderance of physicians in the novel reinforces Segal's medical metaphor. Dr. Stephen Simpson, a former Harvard classmate, is persistent in his efforts to "treat" his friend, inviting Oliver to dinner and arranging dates for him—with yet another doctor, Joanna Stein. While their date is not exactly therapeutic, his inability to respond to Joanna's gentleness and beauty does convince Oliver that he needs the treatment of a specialist. Dr. London, a psychiatrist, is soon probing Oliver's wounds.

Further evidence of Oliver's psychological and emotional state is conveyed in Segal's second metaphorical pattern, the description of his new apartment. After Phil "[despoils] the house of everything that wakened Jenny in the mind" (21), Oliver finds it easy to uproot himself from the rooms he had shared with his wife. His choice of apartment, however, does nothing to convince his father-in-law of his recovery. Located in the "not-quite basement of a brownstone," it is "small and prisonlike," with "iron bars" mounted in the window frames (21). Starkly furnished, it reflects its occupant's mental state, for Oliver lives indeed within the prison of his memories of Jenny. His is a "subterranean" (202) existence.

Segal will extend this house metaphor by attaching it both to Marcie and to the relationship she shares with Oliver, in each case revealing a truth about them. To Oliver, Marcie's residence is a "castle" guarded by a "regiment." The gatekeeper Oliver likens to an "epauletted Cerberus" (126), the three-headed dog of Greek myth that guards the entrance to Hades. The housekeeper is an "ancient crone" (129), an ugly, withered old woman sometimes associated with witchcraft. Behind her palace walls, protected by creatures guaranteed to frighten off all but the most valiant, Marcie, "the princess" (126) or "Queen of Sheba" (127), lives in perfectly appointed splendor. She is untouched and untouchable in the vast expanse of her New York residence, both insulated and isolated from the world of mere mortals. It should not be surprising, then, that a woman who lives such an existence would be oblivious to the impoverished conditions in which her employees in Hong Kong live and work.

Oliver's instinctive response to Marcie's apartment gives evidence of his understanding of his lover's character flaw. Oliver variously describes it as a "museum," a "coliseum" (127), and a "mausoleum" (129). It is a place in which he never feels comfortable. While he, too, may have had a privileged upbringing, one look at the Binnendale bathroom convinces Oliver that Dover House, the Barrett family home, is more a cottage than a castle. Whereas the Barrett bath is "functional and basic," the Binnendale bath is "worthy of a Roman emperor" (135). The note of disapproval in Oliver's description clearly signifies comparable unease with the person who could take for granted such lavishness.

Although Marcie passes "the test of grime," neither she nor Oliver is comfortable in his "rat house" (20). For Oliver, the problem is more than rancid towels, an unmade bed, and the general clutter of law books, dirty dishes, and sweaty socks. Although Jenny never lived in his new apartment, she inhabits it, for "home," Oliver confesses to himself, "is still a place I live with Jenny" (138). To overcome this obstacle in their relationship, Marcie determines that they inhabit what Oliver terms "neutral territory," a place that is neither his nor hers but rather a "DMZ" (200), and she takes the initiative to rent such a place for them. Yet this demilitarized zone also fails to offer more than basic shelter to the couple.

Especially for Oliver, the "dream house" (202) on Eighty-sixth Street is a hollow shell. In its perfection, it is "unreal" (201) and uninhabitable.

Unless Marcie is there with him, Oliver retreats to his basement, where, amid his books, he can think. To him, the dream house will always be "Marcie's new apartment" (202), and he is as lonely there as he was in his dungeon.

Segal's close attention to the spaces his characters inhabit invests them with symbolic significance. They represent their occupants, revealing the contours of their inner selves. More than that, they make visible Marcie and Oliver's essential incompatibility long before their final clash in Hong Kong. It isn't Jenny's ghost that comes between Segal's lovers, but rather their conflicting values—values embodied by their places of residence. Quite simply, they live in different worlds.

The Confidant

Segal relies on another narrative strategy in *Oliver's Story*—the confidant—to convey information about his central character. Because Segal tells Oliver's story from the perspective of the first-person, or "I," narrator, readers are privy to his private thoughts and feelings. To prevent the novel from becoming an interior monologue, however, a narrative that takes place solely within the mind of the narrator, Segal must depend on other strategies of revealing information. Use of the confidant, or person to whom secrets are confided, serves this purpose.

When he has Oliver confide in Phil Cavilleri, his father-in-law, or Dr. London, his therapist, Segal conveys private information both dramatically and realistically. Oliver doesn't just think it; he says and lives it. It is only natural, for instance, that Oliver would share his grief with the other man in Jenny's life, and it is not surprising given his psychic wounds that he would seek the counsel of a specialist. His confessions to these sympathetic listeners thus become dramatic scenes rather than passive reflections, lending a sense of immediacy to the narrative.

In *Love Story*, despite the use of the first-person narrator, such confidants were unnecessary. Oliver's musings breathed life into memory, vivifying Jenny by recreating scenes from their shared life and thereby revealing all about him. In *Oliver's Story*, however, Jenny's absence forces Segal to expand his narrative strategies to convey information. In relying on the confidant, Segal resolves a problem and gives further evidence of his mastery of form.

THEMATIC DEVELOPMENT

Segal signals the central theme of *Oliver's Story* in the epigraph, or quotation, with which the novel begins. The line from Robert Anderson's 1968 drama *I Never Sang for My Father* evokes the theme of resolution, both its difficulty and its importance. Segal's choice of epigraph is important because it indicates the two levels at which the theme operates. At one level, Segal does indeed explore the difficulty and even the impossibility of reconciling a relationship ended by death. Oliver faces that challenge on every page of the novel. At another level, Segal extends in *Oliver's Story* the central theme of *Love Story* by continuing his examination of the father-son relationship. Like Anderson's play, which takes as its subject a middle-aged man's attempts to establish an affectionate connection to his father, *Oliver's Story* ultimately focuses on a young man's reconciliation with both his father and his paternal inheritance. On both levels, then, Segal charts the struggle toward resolution of a relationship. In doing so, he brings a certain measure of closure to the life of Oliver Barrett.

Death may bring an abrupt end to Jenny's life, but it does not sever Oliver's relationship to the woman he loves still. Jenny lives in his memory; her spirit inhabits his home. Other women may replace her, but they cannot displace her, as Oliver's relationship with Marcie makes clear. When their relationship ends, Oliver feels hardly a pang of regret. Marcie had made him feel again, but she had not made him live again. Too often he was lonely in their togetherness. They may have talked, but as Oliver had confessed to Dr. London, they did not communicate (156). Losing Marcie, in other words, simply does not compare to losing Jenny, for in their "constant dialogue," Oliver had discovered himself (157). As the novel's epigraph suggests, Oliver may never resolve his relationship with Jenny, and the novel's final lines reinforce the point. Wondering what his life would be like if Jenny were alive, Oliver acknowledges, "I would also be alive" (256). Oliver has learned to contain his grief, to live with loss, and even to advance into the future. That may be the only resolution he can expect.

Resolution of the father-son relationship in *Oliver's Story* is not complicated by death but rather by a lifetime of misunderstanding and hurt. History, in other words, is the barrier between the Oliver Barretts. That history had been the central focus of *Love Story*. Oliver had disowned his father by choosing to marry Jenny and then had stubbornly opposed all her efforts to mend the breach between them. At Jenny's death, Oliver had found comfort in his father's embrace, a gesture signifying their tentative reconciliation, so as *Oliver's Story* opens, the status of their relationship is in question. Readers immediately know Oliver's response to his wife's death, but they wonder about the effects of the intervening eighteen months on the slender thread connecting father and son. They find that it is frayed but not broken and that ultimately it can be mended.

While their relationship is cordial but not close, no longer does Oliver refer to his father as "Old Stoneyface" or "the Sonovabitch." No longer is his father the focus of his anger and self-doubt. Now it is death and loss and his own selfishness that incense him. Yet the old wounds are barely healed. Oliver confesses that immediately following Jenny's death, he "needed Phil," not his father, "to teach me how to grieve" (15). Eighteen months later, Phil Cavilleri continues to function as a surrogate father to Oliver, urging his son-in-law to move forward in his life without Jenny and even encouraging him to date other women and to marry again. Oliver gets no such counsel from his own father, in whom he confides very little.

Oliver's sessions with Dr. London, his therapist, also reveal that the old emotional scars have not healed. Oliver's first words to his therapist, "Let's begin by leaving out King Oedipus completely" (48), immediately raise the issue of the father-son relationship. The allusion to the ancient Greek tragedy in which a son kills his father and marries his mother, which was a focus of analysis in the previous chapter on *Love Story*, suggests that Oliver's feelings about his own father are still unresolved. Within a week of his first session with Dr. London, Oliver is confessing the ugly truth of his patrimony, a fortune founded on the exploitation of impoverished workers in the family textile mills (53–56). This legacy gives Oliver and his social conscience a reason to distance himself from his father.

Segal also uses Marcie's relationship with her father as an analogue to the Barretts' relationship. Like Oliver, Marcie had never really felt her father's love, and she had longed for his attention and approval: "Every move she ever made in life was always as a challenge or a message to her own Big Daddy" (116–17). As they share their childhood hurts, Oliver finds that they sing the same song of "competition-admiration" (116) for their fathers and, rather surprisingly, that each had played the role of the "Melancholy Prince" (117) in the drama of their lives.

All of this emphasis on fathers makes it clear that *Oliver's Story* will resolve the thematic issues of *Love Story*, and that resolution will occur when Oliver learns that his father is worthy of emulation. On the occasion of his father's sixty-fifth birthday, Oliver flies to Boston to join an office celebration. While everyone sang his father's praises, Oliver "behaved" (250). When James Francis, a representative of the textile workers' union, gave a "testimonial" (251) to his father's goodness, Oliver "just nodded" (251). As Francis proceeds to tell Oliver about his father's efforts to preserve the workers' jobs and to improve their working conditions, even in the face of fierce competition, his words penetrate Oliver's resistance. Looking across the room at his father, Oliver sees "a wholly different person" (252), someone with whom he shares a common bond. He even has to acknowledge that his father has acted on his principles, and not, like Oliver, merely talked about them. This knowledge will prompt Oliver to reevaluate his father and their relationship.

By the novel's end, Oliver understands that there exists an alternative Barrett tradition to which he is connected—through his father. He can thus assume his position in The Firm and join his father in their common efforts. When he does so, Oliver also concludes his search for self. He had "tried to be so many things," he confesses to himself, "just to avoid confronting who I am," but he eventually asserts unequivocally, "I am Oliver Barrett. The Fourth" (253). That saying of self allows Oliver to move forward in life. Five years later, he still grieves for Jenny, but "Barrett that I am" (256), he gains satisfaction from his work and from the "responsibility" (256) that he had once rejected because it was part of his patrimony. The resolution of this conflict is Oliver's real story.

A FEMINIST READING OF *OLIVER'S STORY*

As the allusions to Oedipus and the focus of its theme suggest, *Oliver's Story* could certainly be analyzed from the perspective of the psychological critic. Yet the role and place of women, and particularly of Marcie Nash, in Oliver's life complicate his efforts to assert his identity, and this fact offers fertile ground to the feminist critic, who focuses on an analysis of gender differences and gender expectations in literature. To understand the perspective of such a critic, we need first to consider the word "feminism," a term everyone recognizes but one that few can define clearly and with uniform agreement. Feminist criticism does not include all literary criticism written by women, since not all women are feminists, nor does it include all criticism written by feminists, since they may view a literary work from any theoretical perspective. The characteristic common to feminist criticism is its concern for the impact of gender on reading and writing. To determine that impact, it examines not only the concerns of literature, but also sociological, political, and economic ideas. "The feminist critique," as Elaine Showalter notes, "is essentially political and polemical" ("Poetics" 129), and thus it suggests alternatives to tradition.

Histories of feminist criticism usually divide it into three broad phases. The first involves analysis of patriarchal culture, a term for the institutions, attitudes, and beliefs of a society dominated by men. In the field of literary criticism, this analysis or critique exposes what Showalter calls "the misogyny of literary practice," the explicit and implicit prejudices in male writing about women. Such practices include, according to Showalter, "the stereotyped images of women in literature as angels or monsters, the literary abuse or textual harassment of women in classics and popular male literature, and the exclusion of women from literary history" ("Revolution" 5). This feminist critique examines as well the woman as reader of works by men and by other women, exploring the way in which "the hypothesis of a female reader changes our apprehension of" the literary text ("Poetics" 128).

This feminist critique has led to enlightening new interpretations of classics previously evaluated only by male critics with traditional attitudes. Some critics, however, caution against the potential dangers of such readings, arguing that the social and historical contexts of a literary work are essential to understanding the author's choices. For example, it is unfair for a contemporary feminist critic to berate Chaucer for failing to make the Wife of Bath a lawyer because women professionals did not exist in his time. But when applied to modern and contemporary works of literature, this feminist critique yields some surprising debate as both male and female critics comment on the same work—frequently with remarkably different conclusions.

The second phase of feminist literary criticism has been termed "gynocriticism," or a concern with women as writers giving expression to the female experience through their work ("Poetics" 128–29). Discovering that women writers had a literature of their own, gynocritics set out to map the territory of the female imagination. They sought to define the distinctive mode of discourse, or means of communication, that distinguished women's texts from men's. This focus led to the recovery of many forgotten works by women. It led as well to a new understanding of the struggles women writers faced to express their own visions and experiences in a patriarchal society that discounted them.

Both of these aspects of feminism constitute what in recent years has been termed "gender studies." Both also share the idea that gender difference determines much about a person's life experience and thus about one's means of communicating, reading, or writing. A third phase of feminism focuses on the similarities between men and women and argues that emphasizing differences is a tactic used by men to exclude and oppress women. These critics stress instead the humanity of all people, regardless of gender. They believe that the only way to achieve equality is to deny that fundamental differences between men and women exist. In fact, these egalitarian feminists fear that the emphasis on difference weakens feminism because it produces a kind of reverse discrimination and stereotyping—everything male is negative, and everything female is positive. The egalitarian feminists believe that the narrow focus of gender studies critics leads to their isolation in the critical debate and thus their effectual silencing. Consequently, they promote the shared experience of all people as the foundation of real equality and understanding.

Whatever their critical stance, feminists do seem to share one important idea about literary criticism: the impossibility of achieving objectivity. For years, critics believed that the author's personal history, the social expectations of his or her time, and the historical events that transpired during the author's life had no bearing on understanding literary works. Instead, literature was a world of its own, complete in itself, and thus could be evaluated without reference to personal, social, and historical context. Feminist critics believe that such objectivity is impossible. Instead, they promote subjectivity—responses based on experience and belief. They recognize that every reader brings both aspects to the literary work and thus understands literature from a personal perspective.

From a feminist perspective, *Oliver's Story*, for all its pretensions of being modern and liberal, is a misogynistic work. Despite its language and situations, its view of women is archaic. Jenny, its image of the perfect woman, is the angel in the house so admired in a previous century. Marcie, the image of the liberated woman, is, according to Oliver, "a cold and heartless bitch" (245) who must ultimately be punished for daring to act like a man. And Oliver, as the symbol of patriarchal authority, takes comfort in the status quo and does everything he can to preserve it. He is a tradition-bound Barrett in every way.

On the surface, *Oliver's Story* seems to advance the changing mores and social patterns of its time, particularly in its treatment of women's roles and sexual relationships. Both Joanna Stein and Marcie Nash are professional women actively engaged in the practice of their careers. Sexually liberated, Marcie is as much pursuer of as pursued by Oliver. In fact, she sends him flowers (122), and she eventually even proposes marriage to him (221). She and Oliver establish a "modern" (151) relationship, each of them working outside the home, sharing responsibilities, respecting the other's individuality. Yet almost from the beginning, a tone of complaint makes clear Oliver's dissatisfaction with their situation. Liberal he may be, especially when it comes to defending the rights of others, but in his own life, Oliver is definitely not modern.

Basically, Oliver is chauvinistic. He patronizes and belittles women to reinforce his own sense of self, and he simply cannot accept assertive women. In fact, his relationship with Marcie is born of a desire to "humiliate" (64) a woman who has dared to challenge his superiority. As he confesses to Dr. London prior to his tennis match with Marcie, "I love to put aggressive women down" (66). When they meet at the Gotham Tennis Club, Oliver clearly intends to gain control of the woman who had parried his every thrust on the jogging path the day before.

Oliver's tendency to treat Marcie as a sex object is yet another indication of his chauvinism. One of the first things he notices about the woman jogging ahead of him, the woman who turns out to be Marcie, is her "fantastic ass" (58). Later, when Oliver goes to her apartment for the first time, he will propose a toast to Marcie's "tits and ass" (128). Marcie will reproach him for being "crude" and then acquiesce with a laugh, thereby excusing his language and gesture. But her acceptance of such treatment does not diminish its significance. Like some adolescent boy, Oliver still views women as body parts, not as full human beings. The size of their breasts, not their brains, is what matters to him.

Given Oliver's sexist attitudes, his rejection of Marcie is not surprising. She is, after all, everything that makes him uncomfortable about women. He gets "annoyed" when Marcie insists on driving his Porsche, fast, and when she chooses the time and place of what he intends to be his seduction of her (88). He also gets irritated when she rents and furnishes "their" apartment. As he complains to Dr. London, "She likes to . . . manage both our lives" (201). When business prevents Marcie from attending a Thanksgiving celebration, Phil attempts to ease Oliver's palpable disappointment by discussing the duties of a wife and urging marriage (185). Shortly thereafter, Oliver devises a test of Marcie's commitment:

He asks her to sell the stores, which Marcie refuses to do. Oliver tries. He even gives this woman who lacks all domestic skills a copy of *The Joy of Cooking* as a Christmas present (214). But he cannot transform this independent person into the woman he needs and wants. He cannot transform her into Jenny.

Jenny, of course, had been the perfect woman. She and Oliver may have shared fewer common bonds than Marcie and Oliver do, but as a result, they were learning and growing together (156–58). Jenny, unlike Marcie, needed her husband, and she understood that Oliver needed to be needed. She was, therefore, willing to sacrifice her career to his because it was, in effect, their career, their goal. Oliver really does not want a "modern" relationship. He wants instead what he had with Jenny. As if speaking for his daughter, Phil describes it: "A man an' a woman gotta *cleave* together" (185).

Oliver would, and does, deny his chauvinism. On several occasions he deliberately mentions women's liberation as if to prove to himself (and readers) that he is sensitive to the changing role of women (51; 150) and therefore not a sexist. Such protestations, however, ring hollow when sounded against his actions. Oliver may convince himself that moral scruples are behind his break with Marcie, but she knows that Hong Kong sweatshops have nothing to do with it (244). Oliver breaks with Marcie because she is ambitious and assertive, because she does not need him. He breaks with Marcie because he is a Barrett, because he is linked to tradition. Five years later, when the novel ends, he is even contemplating marriage to a "distant cousin" (255).

If self-knowledge and acceptance of the paternal legacy are central to the drama of resolution in *Oliver's Story*, then one of the things Oliver must finally acknowledge about himself is his own paternalism. Whether it is a desire to care for the woman he loves or to defend the rights of the dispossessed and disadvantaged, traditional values motivate Oliver. Traditional values make him what he is—a Barrett. With that assertion, Oliver's story ends.

5

Man, Woman and Child
(1980)

With his third novel, *Man, Woman and Child* (1980), Erich Segal ventured into new territory. Gone for the first time in Segal's writing career was Oliver Barrett IV, his story having been charted in *Love Story* and its sequel, *Oliver's Story*. A new hero was about to enter an old world, where he would play out an old story. "Europe," as R. Z. Sheppard noted in a review of the novel, would be "the seducer of American innocence" (92), and the lives of one family would never be the same. The loss of innocence would provide Segal with a new theme to explore, new ground to cover, and in recording his findings, he attempted some new narrative strategies as well.

Man, Woman and Child is rather a misnomer, for the novel actually focuses on man, woman, and three children. The Beckwiths, Bob and Sheila, are the perfect married couple. He is a noted professor at Massachusetts Institute of Technology; she is a successful editor at Harvard University Press. After nearly twenty years of marriage, they have two lovely daughters, a home in Lexington, Massachusetts, and a summer place on Cape Cod. College sweethearts, they have "a marriage very much in sync" (11) until a nine-year-old boy enters their lives and breaks their rhythm.

Ten years before the events in the novel, Bob had attended a professional conference in the south of France. It was 1968, during a period of social and political unrest, and Bob, an innocent abroad, found himself in the middle of a confrontation with a *gendarme*. When the policeman strikes him on the head with his club, he is rescued by the beautiful young doctor whose honor he had tried to defend. She treats his wounds and offers him amends. Seduced by France, Bob succumbs to the charms of Nicole Guérin and then, following a weekend of passion, returns to his ordinary life. Ten years later his brief affair is "so well suppressed [that] he almost had convinced himself it never happened" (3). But when Nicole is killed in an auto accident, Bob must face the truth of his past in the shape of Jean-Claude Guérin—his son. Man, woman, and children must now negotiate the twisted paths of conflicting emotions and reconfigure the pattern of their lives.

NARRATIVE STRATEGIES: FLASHBACKS, POINT OF VIEW, AND THE CONFIDANT

The "narrative technique" in *Man, Woman and Child* is still, as Sheppard observes, "more cinematic than literary" (92). Short, episodic chapters tend to emphasize plot over character, and physical description is minimal. The novel tends, in other words, to telegraph its points rather than expound on them. Yet it also gives evidence of Segal's increasing command of different narrative strategies, especially in his construction of plot and his use of point of view.

Flashbacks

The opening scene of *Man, Woman and Child* plunges the Beckwiths into immediate crisis. A telephone call from France brings Bob the news of Nicole's death and Jean-Claude's existence, turning his perfect world into chaos. Because the Beckwith crisis can only be understood within the context of the past, Segal had to determine a strategy for conveying past events to readers. He could, of course, have simply related them in a passage of narrative exposition, or straightforward explanation. His choice, however, was to dramatize the events, and to do so, he relied upon the flashback, a device by which an author presents material that occurred prior to the opening scene of the work.

Segal had used the device in his previous novels. The plot of *Love Story*, in fact, which begins with the announcement of Jenny's death, is basically an extended flashback. In *Man, Woman and Child*, however, the placement of the flashbacks is more deliberate and interrupts the logical sequence of events. The disruptions draw attention to the flashbacks, thereby suggesting that they are intended not simply to provide information, but also to serve as counterpoints to key events in the novel's present.

Twice Segal flashes back to the past, and both sequences take the form of Bob's dramatized recollections. The first episode occurs in chapters 6 through 8, when Bob recalls his courtship of Sheila and their first happy years of marriage through the birth of their first child. Readers see the romance between a painfully inept Romeo and an equally shy Juliet blossom overnight into a perfect specimen of love. Matched in temperament, values, and goals, the Beckwiths have never had to struggle in their married life, nor have they faced any real test of their commitment to each other. Yet as the first five chapters of the novel make clear, the foundation of their perfect marriage is cracked. They must either repair the damage or erect a new structure.

The second flashback occurs late in the novel in chapters 27 through 30, when Jean-Claude's medical emergency reminds Bob of his own ten years before. Readers finally learn the secret so deeply buried in Bob's subconscious that it is hardly even a memory anymore. They meet for the first time Nicole Guérin, the vibrant, unconventional woman who stirred unknown passions in Bob, and see dramatized the circumstances of their brief affair. Segal deliberately withholds this information from readers until the novel's end not only to prolong the mystery of this crucial incident but also to enhance its significance. When this final piece of the puzzle completes the picture, readers have the full context of the Beckwith marriage.

Point of View

In addition to developing his use of the flashback, Segal also experiments in *Man, Woman and Child* with point of view, or the perspective from which an author tells a story. Segal had employed a first-person, or "I," narrator in his previous novels, thereby limiting his focus to his central character. In his third novel, however, he uses an omniscient narrator. The author, in other words, serves as a seemingly all-knowing maker who can relate the thoughts and feelings of any character. The omniscient narrator, unlike the first-person narrator, also has unrestricted knowledge of events. He or she need not witness or be a participant in the action in order to relate it to readers.

Use of an omniscient narrator broadens the scope of Segal's novel. Readers learn not only Bob's feelings about the crisis in his life, but also Sheila's response to her husband's infidelity. They witness his growing attachment to his young son and Sheila's struggle to recapture her self-esteem because the omniscient narrator can relate the actions and reactions of husband and wife as well as that of daughters and son.

The Confidant

One other narrative device—the confidant—is important to the development of *Man, Woman and Child*. The confidant is a character who takes little part in the action of the story but is close to the protagonist and receives the confidences and intimate thoughts of the central character. In *Man, Woman and Child*, Bernie Ackerman functions as Bob's confidant while Sheila's confidante is Margo van Nostrand. Both share long and intimate friendships with their former college classmates, so it is not surprising that Bob and Sheila turn to them for advice and comfort during their family crisis, especially since the situation has made it virtually impossible to talk to each other.

Sheila, for instance, who has stoically invited Jean-Claude into their home, has had to suppress her hurt and anger to keep the family peace, but to Margo, she can give vent to her feelings and take comfort from her friend's sympathy and support. Overwhelmed by guilt for the pain he has caused his family, Bob must conceal the pride and love he feels for his son, but to Bernie, he can give voice to his complicated and conflicting emotions. The exchanges with the confidants allow Segal to reveal essential information in a realistic way, without having to resort to authorial intrusion.

CHARACTER DEVELOPMENT

Despite the emotional turmoil into which the Beckwith family is tossed by the knowledge of Bob's infidelity and Jean-Claude's existence, the characters themselves are rather thinly drawn. Knowledge, in other words, may chasten them, but it does not greatly change them. Their marriage, their family, are tested, but the binding ties of love and their own essential goodness and strength of character ultimately reunite man, woman, and children.

Robert Beckwith, the novel's central character, is a man who deals in facts, yet he has avoided for ten years one of the key facts of his own life—his infidelity. An esteemed professor of statistics at MIT, he lives a neatly ordered life that is the envy of friends and colleagues. Indeed, he seems to have everything that he could possibly want, both personal satisfaction and professional recognition. The one key fact that he has so conveniently forgotten, however, reveals another side of Bob Beckwith, a desire for something more than he has. Jean-Claude becomes the embodiment of that desire. His son is the second self that neither Jessica nor Paula can ever be for their father, and the fact that Jean-Claude represents his one unconventional act makes him that much more his father's son.

Until he learns of Jean-Claude's existence, Bob has never confronted his disappointment about not having a son, so it had made no sense to long for the impossible. Jean-Claude, however, is a fact, and his reality allows Bob to admit his desire. He would like to be the father of a *"quarterback"* (16). He would like to have a reason to play in the Ackermans' annual father-son softball game. He would like to know the pride that Bernie feels watching his son, David, excel on the soccer field. From the moment Bob meets Jean-Claude, he finds it difficult and then impossible to think of losing this extension of himself.

Fatherhood is clearly important to Bob. In fact, the early scenes of the novel establish him as an active, loving father to his two daughters. Twelve-year-old Jessica has reached the age at which she no longer idolizes her father yet still seeks his recognition and approval (36). Nine-year-old Paula quite simply adores her father; no other man could take his place. Yet no other episode in the novel makes Bob feel more like a father than the day he spends with Jean-Claude prior to what is supposed to be the child's banishment to France.

On that day, Bob first takes his son to his office at MIT, where the boy sits in his father's chair, a miniature Professor Beckwith (158), and then to the Museum of Science, where Jean-Claude confides dreams and secrets to his father (159–61). To prolong the day and ensure that his son will miss the flight to France, Bob then takes him to a Boston Pops concert, where he grows nostalgic about his own father (163). Bob's "best hope" has been that his son "would like me—no, love me, imperfect as

I am" (145). On what is to be their last day together, Bob knows that his dream is a reality. On that day, he really understands the meaning of fatherhood.

For Sheila, who knows and understands her husband perhaps better than he knows himself, Jean-Claude is the embodiment of her deepest fears. Unable to bear other children, she has trusted Bob's reassurances "that what they shared was far too strong for anything to change" (17). But knowledge of his infidelity shatters that trust, and the reality of Jean-Claude rekindles old insecurities. As Margo tells her, "You've always been the perfect wife and you've just had your ego flattened with a steam roller" (127). Sheila invites the boy into their home not as a gesture of compassion toward an innocent orphan but rather to save her marriage. (Her maiden name may be Goodhart, but even the kindest people can be selfish when they need to be.) She understands that if she denies Bob this chance to know his son she risks losing him at some point in the future. She is neither brave nor generous, she confesses to Bob when he praises her sacrifice. She is "just thirty-nine-years-old" (27). The tone of defeat in that admission is unmistakable.

Jean-Claude's presence in their home tests Sheila's strength and resolve. At times the situation is more than she can bear, so she escapes into work and seeks comfort from her friend Margo. She even considers having an affair with Gavin Wilson, the "intellectual pinup" (154) whose book she is editing. Her sadness and suffering, however, rather ironically connect her to the child who has caused her pain and who silently suffers his own (100), and because she does, in fact, have a good heart, she finds herself responding to Jean-Claude's need.

If fatherhood is important to Bob, then motherhood is equally important to Sheila. In fact, a mother's instinct to care for a child also prompts Sheila to develop a grudging attachment to the boy, but when his presence threatens her own children, Sheila asserts their rights and demands that Bob send him back to France. So long as her daughters think that Jean-Claude is simply a guest, Sheila can bear her own hurt, but when they learn that their guest is their half brother, Jessica and Paula fear losing their father. To protect her daughters, Sheila will once again be selfish.

Their shared commitment to motherhood and fatherhood is ultimately the ground on which Sheila and Bob reestablish their marriage. When Jean-Claude is hospitalized for an emergency appendectomy and nearly dies of peritonitis, the Beckwiths act together to save his life and then to help him recuperate not only from the trauma of surgery but also from the emotional wounds that they have inflicted on him. Having first banished him back to France, Sheila, who has grown genuinely fond of the child, now insists that Jean-Claude return to their home. She will not shirk her responsibility to a motherless child. Moreover, as she tells Bob, with Jean-Claude in their lives, "instead of somewhere in the corner of everyone's imagination," they have a "better chance" (210) of saving their marriage and preserving their family. Bob, she knows, must not be forced to choose between his children because as their father he has obligations to them all. In being parents to all their children—Jessica, Paula, and Jean-Claude—the Beckwiths thus reconnect to the best parts of themselves, the love and compassion, the deep sense of responsibility, that made them the perfect couple and can do so again.

THEMATIC DEVELOPMENT

The crisis in the Beckwith marriage is a direct consequence of a betrayal of trust, a lapse in values prompted by contact with another and different set of values. This encounter, embodied first in Nicole and Bob and then in Jean-Claude and the Beckwiths, reveals the theme, or central idea, of *Man, Woman and Child*. When Bob finds himself in the south of France floating naked in the sea with a beautiful woman, "thousands of miles from all his values" (192), he will face a moral crisis, and so, too, will all the Beckwiths when Jean-Claude enters their home. Each of them will be tested, and all of them will be stripped of illusions about themselves and others. As the novel's epigraph by the Irish poet William Butler Yeats suggests, "The ceremony of innocence is drowned" in the experience.

The conflict of cultures through international experience has been a traditional theme in literature. American writers generally dramatize the theme as a conflict between sophisticated, rather cynical Europeans and naive, rather optimistic Americans. The Americans are eager to experience a culture frequently perceived as superior to their own, and they trust in the natives' good will and good conduct. That trust, however, is frequently misplaced. More often than not, the Americans are deceived by European manners, assuming that they are a sign of high moral principle when in fact they conceal moral decadence. Because they misunderstand appearances, they find themselves seduced and betrayed and ultimately disillusioned. American innocence is sacrificed, in other words, to European sophistication. This international theme shapes the plots of Nathaniel Hawthorne's *The Marble Faun* and many of the novels of Henry James, including *Daisy Miller*, *The American*, and *The Portrait of a Lady*. Ernest Hemingway, F. Scott Fitzgerald, and other modern and contemporary authors also draw on this theme. In *Man, Woman and Child*, Segal works within this tradition as well.

Almost from the moment he steps off the plane, Bob finds himself seduced by Europe. His colleague and traveling companion, however, is immune to its charms, so while Bob marvels at the splendors of the Pyrennes and the beauty of the Mediterranean, Herb Harrison talks academic politics, oblivious to anything but his own ego. When Bob wants to stop for a brief visit at an ancient cathedral, Herb balks at the suggestion (175), and later he warns of dire consequences when Bob proposes exploring the cobbled streets of Sète on his own (176). Herb's provincialism almost prevents Bob's seduction, but Bob does not wish to be saved. Until this point in his life, he has been utterly conventional. College, career, marriage, family have followed in predictable sequence, but now, Bob is eager to experience another culture, eager, in fact, for experience.

Nicole Guérin embodies that culture, especially its unconventionality. Bob tells her that he "believe[s] in marriage" (191) and thus, by implication, the values associated with it—trust, commitment, honor. In contrast, Nicole values her independence and self-sufficiency. She has no desire to marry, although she would someday like to be a mother (190). Like everything else that Bob encounters in France, including student riots and Sète's revolutionary mayor, Nicole challenges him to lose control (191), and eventually he does indeed give himself up to experience. In effect, France's revolutionary spirit releases the spring of Bob's own desire.

Bob's seduction by Europe is a metaphorical fall from grace. At one point in the novel, Margo has attempted to reassure Sheila of Bob's fidelity by telling her, "He thinks he's Adam and you're Eve" (79), and indeed, for Bob and Sheila it has been as if they were the only man and woman in the world and that world was paradise. But like Adam, who is tempted to sin and does, Bob betrays a trust and falls from innocence to experience. Because he keeps his indiscretion a secret, even eventually from himself, Bob is not immediately expelled from his paradise. But when his secret is revealed, "things fall apart," as the novel's epigraph indicates, and nothing will be the same again for anybody. Paradise is lost.

Bob's experience will be recapitulated to some degree by every member of his family. Sheila, for instance, will be tempted to betray her marriage vows by Gavin Wilson, an emissary from that other world. The British-born, former Oxford don is witty and urbane, and his position as a foreign policy expert on the National Security Council carries the cachet of power and prestige. His cosmopolitanism is certainly an attraction to Sheila. Bruised and hurting from the blow to her self-esteem, she is flattered that a man such as Gavin finds her desirable, but ultimately she does not succumb to his charms. Yet the fact that she seriously considers surrendering her values causes Sheila to recognize how Bob could have lapsed from his and to question her own strength of character. She, too, in other words, falls into knowledge through her cosmopolitan encounter.

Jessica and Paula are eager to embrace their foreign guest, for Jean-Claude brings with him the scent of the exotic and the lure of the unique. For Jessica especially, Jean-Claude's visit promises an opportunity not only to practice her French but also to escape the provincialism of her native land. Just as she is lamenting "another summer with my bourgeois family on tedious Cape Cod" (10), Jessica gets her wish, the chance "to gain worldliness through international experience" (27). If she cannot go to France, it can come to her in the guise of a nine-year-old boy.

Initially, Jean-Claude disappoints neither of the girls. He is diplomatic enough to avoid entanglement in the girls' sibling rivalry, and his curious customs, such as drinking coffee rather than milk in the morning (62), and unconventional tastes earn an approving "Cool" from a delighted Paula (86). When Jean-Claude helps the girls prepare a surprise dinner for Sheila, they cook up a fast friendship in addition to a veal stew.

Eventually, however, the girls learn that Jean-Claude is more than a Gallic poster boy, and the knowledge is devastating. Paula, too young to understand the significance of Jean-Claude's existence, lives in constant fear that her father will desert her for his son (210). Jessica, on the verge of her own sexual awakening, distances herself from the man who betrayed her as well as her mother (198). Jean-Claude's *difference* is no longer quaint and appealing to them, but rather vulgar and threatening. It represents—indeed, he represents—attitudes and behaviors too fearsome to contemplate, but Jessica and Paula have already done so and they will never be the same. Nor will Jean-Claude, against whom the girls hurl their hurt, anger, and fear when they learn of his relationship to them (135). He finds and loses a family through no fault of his own but rather for all that he embodies. Their innocence has been stripped from them too soon.

The knowledge of imperfection and the loss of innocence are at the core of *Man, Woman and Child*. In fact, as Sheila tells her daughters, "the most painful part of growing up is discovering that nobody's perfect. Not even your parents" (147). Everyone in the novel has to accept this fact about others and about themselves. The vehicle to that knowledge is the cosmopolitan encounter, contact with foreign values and culture that raises fundamental questions about their own beliefs and lifestyles. International experience is indeed broadening, and the Beckwiths will never be the same for it.

A CULTURAL CRITIQUE OF *MAN, WOMAN AND CHILD*

The cross-cultural encounters in *Man, Woman and Child* give Segal the opportunity to dissect contemporary society and to offer some rather insightful cultural criticism. If we view it as a sociological document, the novel records and reflects the attitudes and behaviors of the people who inhabit the world it re-creates. Thus, the critic may examine it as an expression of culture. This critical perspective looks back to Matthew Arnold's view that literature offers a critique of life. It also bears some connection to Marxism, with its emphasis on the material foundation of a culture's ideology. It is not, however, specifically Marxist, being more appropriately linked to a tradition of American liberalism devoted not so much to doctrine or methodology as to cultural commentary.

While the field of cultural studies is not new, its recognition as a unique branch of inquiry is a relatively recent development, primarily identified with postmodernism. In other words, it has come into its own since the end of the Second World War. Generally, cultural critics apply the concepts and theories of various disciplines to the elite arts, popular culture, the media, ordinary life, and other aspects of contemporary culture and society. Cultural criticism is, according to Arthur Asa Berger, "a multidisciplinary, interdisciplinary, pandisciplinary, or meta-disciplinary undertaking" (2). Consequently, it may involve literary theory, psychoanalytic theory, Marxist theory, sociological and anthropological theory. Whatever their approach or discipline, however, cultural critics seek to understand their culture and society and to explain it to those who live in it.

While this definition of cultural criticism may seem rather broad, containing so much that it cannot be contained itself, one important concept gives shape to this critical approach. Cultural criticism, as Berger notes, "is always grounded in some perspective on things that the critic ... believes best explains things" (8). In other words, cultural critics always have some connection to, or identify themselves with, a group or discipline. Some are feminists, some Marxists, some conservatives, radicals, Freudians, anthropologists, or any combination of these or other groups. For the purposes of this analysis of *Man, Woman and Child*, then, we shall approach the novel from a sociohistorical perspective that has much in common with Marxism, a theory explained in chapter 6, but which is not specifically Marxist.

If we examine *Man, Woman and Child* as a social and historical document, we discover that it is essentially a novel of manners, that is, one that focuses on the social customs, manners, conventions, and habits of a definite social class at a particular time and place, frequently in a comic or satiric view. In other words, it uses humor or sarcasm to expose and ridicule human vices and follies. As a novel of manners, *Man, Woman and Child* exposes the superficiality and provincialism of middle-class America and thus lays it open to the critique of life that is cultural criticism.

Marriage is, of course, one of the institutions placed under the microscope in the novel. The Beckwiths' marriage, for example, has always been the envy of their friends, so news of Bob's affair is both shocking and disillusioning. Margo van Nostrand, Sheila's confidante, is clearly distressed by the "shattering [of] *her* remaining illusions" (80) about fidelity in marriage. Equally troubled is Bernie Ackerman, who confides in Bob that it was the model of the Beckwith marriage that once kept him from adultery (95). As Bernie tells Bob, "You and Sheila were like those little figures on a wedding cake" (94), the very ideal of the happily married couple.

As Bernie's comparison suggests, however, that ideal is as artificial and unrealistic as those wedding cake figures. In real life, even the best marriages fall victim to human imperfection, and with increasing frequency, the marital history of Margo Fulton Andrews Bedford van Nostrand is the norm. Her first marriage lasted only sixteen months (56); an affair ended her second (80). Now the thrice-married Margo adds spice to her predictable life with Hal by engaging in harmless, but flattering flirtations (78). Fidelity in marriage, it seems, is an ideal that very few can attain.

Segal's novel also exposes the decidedly masculine bias of middle-class America. Here the emphasis on sports is particularly telling. The Ackermans' annual father-son softball game, for instance, makes Bob feel his failure as a man, for as the father of two daughters, he plays by default rather than by membership in the club. On another occasion, Bernie sympathetically urges Bob to enroll his girls in sports programs so that he will have a reason to be proud of them (90–91). Later, when Bob discovers that Jean-Claude excels on the soccer field, he does indeed feel vindicated as a father (109). Moreover, Jean-Claude's athletic ability transforms him from "Sissy Frenchie Fruitcake" (108) into "Johnny" (206) almost overnight. Sports even belong to American courtship rituals. When Bob, for example, attends the mixer at which he meets Sheila, he covers his scrawny physique behind a football tie (41). Similarly, Davey Ackerman believes that he will win Jessica if she will only "recognize his many athletic virtues" (65). Masculinity, epitomized by athletic prowess and the competitive drive, is clearly at the center of the Beckwith world. Twelve-year-old Jessica may not be the most experienced social critic, but she may be among the most astute when she pronounces, "American men are absolutely driven by ambition. It's what makes them so provincial" (20).

Academia is another of the institutions that comes under scrutiny in *Man, Woman and Child*, and the picture Segal draws of it is not very flattering. While Bob may be both enlightened and esteemed, his professional colleagues, exemplified by P. Herbert Harrison, are a petty lot. Obsessed by academic politics, Harrison, "a pompous ass with lengthy and dissenting views on everything" (11), lacks any intellectual curiosity. Ten years before, when he and Bob had traveled together to their professional conference in France, he had ignored the country's aesthetic delights and cultural charms, so busy was he carping about the mediocrity of his colleagues and the slight to him as senior member of the department in Bob's selection as chairman (175). Harrison's petty complaints and lack of interest in anything beyond his own life subtly condemn the American professorate, which should exemplify intellectual vigor and rigor. Indeed, the education of many of the Americans in the novel appears shallow in comparison to that of their European counterparts.

Nicole Guérin, for instance, who had studied in the United States (and enjoyed the experience immensely), converses as fluently about poetry as she does about pathology. Jean-Claude, who spends much of his time at the Beckwith home reading world history, seems far more experienced and knowledgeable than his counterpart Paula. Even Sète's mayor, Louis Venarguès, is as passionate about world affairs as provincial politics. The Europeans in the novel all seem to look beyond their narrow horizons to the distant expanses. The Americans, in contrast, seem to care passionately only about sports, and they gain their knowledge of the world around them from *Psychology Today* or other pop psychology books such as *Passages* (79).

Finally, in comparison to the style and attitudes embodied by Nicole, middle-class American life looks stultifying and conventional, just the sort of existence that might prompt men and women to desire something else in their lives. Marriage, children, career follow as predictably as the moon follows the sun in the lives of people such as the Beckwiths and the Ackermans. The predictability breeds a sense of deceptive security, a smug conviction that life will be "unchanged, unchanging and unchangeable" (67), thinks Sheila at one point. Manners and mores in such a culture seem more a matter of habit than of deeply held belief. Characters take for granted that their lives will "always" follow the plotted route, so they are unprepared for the uncharted detours.

Life in France, in contrast, seems utterly unpredictable. Residents of Sète find a reason to celebrate any occasion—"the day's catch, the revolution—or maybe just life," Nicole explained to Bob (187). And they accept the unconventional. When Bob expresses surprise about Nicole's "avant-garde" intention to have a child but never to marry, she acknowledges that her life will be "unbourgeois" (190). She does not intend to conform to middle-class values and mores, but then "Sète," she observes, "is certainly not bourgeois" (191). Sète, in other words, gives Nicole the freedom to be herself. She can refuse a post in Paris to run a small clinic in her native village because, as the "blue-jeaned physician" (180) tells Bob, "I live by my own definitions" (186). Bob, in contrast, who is never quite able to explain the reason for his affair (not even to himself) (38; 94), seems never to have really thought about his.

Family relationships are clearly only one aspect of *Man, Woman and Child*. By internationalizing its plot, characters, and setting, Segal places the novel within a tradition that examines as its central theme the loss of innocence. The international element also exposes some provocative contrasts between European and American cultures, thus transforming the work into a novel of manners. In its major elements, then, in plot, theme, and narrative strategies especially, *Man, Woman and Child* gives evidence of Segal's development as a writer. In fact, this will be his last "little" novel, for with his next book, *The Class*, Segal will launch into the first of four expansive novels far different in scope from his first three best-sellers.

6

The Class
(1985)

Erich Segal's 1985 best-seller, *The Class*, marks in both scope and focus a significant departure for the novelist. Whereas his previous novels had concentrated on the life of a single protagonist, or central character, *The Class* weaves together the stories of five Harvard classmates from their first days as undergraduates to their class reunion twenty-five years later. Whereas those previous novels had been limited in scope, *The Class* ranges wide in time, place, and event. It moves from the ivy-covered bricks of Harvard to the glittering stages of New York, the halls of power in Washington, D.C., the holy lands of the Middle East, and encompasses the political, social, and historical changes of a quarter century. Yet for all its epic proportions, *The Class* shares an essential element with at least one of its predecessors. Like *Love Story*, it, too, is basically a coming-of-age story, charting its protagonists' paths to maturity. As Susan Isaacs observes, it examines "how they were shaped by their years at college and what happened to them after they left" (9). In doing so, *The Class* also explores the nature and meaning of success.

The Class may be the most personal of all Segal's novels, for like his characters, Segal is a 1958 graduate of Harvard who attended his twenty-fifth-year class reunion in 1983. In fact, it was the memorial service at that reunion, as he told an interviewer, that helped him find a focus for a novel about his Harvard experience he had wanted to write since 1977. "I went, ready to be satirical," he confessed. "I thought the reunion would be backslapping and drunkenness. It was neither" (Smith 41). Instead, the reunion's memorial service prompted Segal to "take stock" (Smith 45), to come to terms with his own life just as his characters come to terms with theirs. "This book," Segal revealed, "was a real voyage of self-discovery for me. I drew upon my own life for all these characters" (Smith 45).

CHARACTERIZATION

Five members of Harvard's class of 1958 are the focus of Segal's fourth novel. Each has his own history and follows his own future. Yet all are in some ways stereotypes intended to represent the Harvard tradition of the best and the brightest. As representatives of their types, all are rather one-dimensional. Segal telegraphs each character's essential quality in an epigraph, an introductory quotation, written by some of Harvard's famous alumni.

Andrew Eliot is the "preppie." Like Oliver Barrett in *Love Story*, he is descended from a line of colonial forefathers whose ties to Harvard go back to its founding, and also, like Oliver, he finds this family heritage a heavy burden. The son of privilege, a product of exclusive preparatory, or prep, schools, Andrew understands that he is expected to uphold the Eliot tradition of achievement. Yet he seriously doubts his ability to fulfill this obligation. In fact, as the epigraph from "The Love-Song of J. Alfred Prufrock," by the American poet T. S. Eliot, class of 1910, suggests, self-doubt is the hallmark of Andrew's character. He will never be the hero in the drama of his life (20). His doubts, of course, are not unfounded. The advantages of birth and wealth cannot entirely compensate for average intelligence. Nor do they guarantee the drive and ambition to succeed. When Andrew Eliot graduates from Harvard, nobody is more surprised than he (189).

What Andrew lacks in self-confidence and self-direction he more than makes up for in goodness and generosity of spirit. When Ted Lambros needs a place to bring his girlfriend, Andrew allows him to use his room—and bed. When George Keller, a midterm arrival, needs a roommate, Andrew agrees to share his suite with this intensely driven student with whom he has nothing in common. Andrew's sense of noblesse oblige is utterly genuine, and it endears him to his Harvard classmates, making him their trusted confidant. He is, "in *human* terms, the best man in the class" (529).

Ted Lambros, one of the beneficiaries of Andrew's kindness, is *The Class*'s "townie." He is also, admits Segal, the character most like him: "There's a lot of me in Ted," Segal told an interviewer (Smith 45). The son of Greek immigrants, Ted had grown up within sight of Harvard's hallowed halls and had dreamed of one day being part of its traditions. Admission to the university, however, does not guarantee acceptance. Because he lacks the financial means to live in a dormitory, Ted, a classics student, must commute between campus and his parents' home. He must juggle his studies of Greek and Latin with his job at the family restaurant, situated just at the edge of campus, its location a constant symbol of his peripheral status. Fearing that he will ever be relegated to straddling the boundary between two worlds, his dream always within sight but just beyond reach, Ted will devote his career to becoming one of Harvard's "old boys." His quest, to "not disappoint myself" (17), as the epigraph by the American writer Henry David Thoreau, class of 1837, suggests, is a noble one. Yet as the second epigraph, by the American essayist Ralph Waldo Emerson, class of 1821, indicates, it will make this otherwise "sensible" person "selfish" (17).

The Class's Big Man on Campus and representative "jock" is Jason Gilbert, a blonde Apollo (13) whose prowess on the squash and tennis courts makes him the envy of his classmates, the heartthrob of every coed. The all-American boy, Jason is destined for easy success, and his character, as the epigraph by the American poet e. e. cummings, class of 1915, indicates, makes him deserving of the attainment (13). He is admired because he is admirable, because he has the ability to inspire others by his innate sense of justice. Yet one insurmountable obstacle blocks his path. The son of thoroughly assimilated Jewish parents, Jason finds that the world will not ignore his ethnic and religious heritage. During his affluent, suburban boyhood, Jason had been insulated from the sting of prejudice, but entry into the larger world causes him to feel its bite daily. In fact, Jason's place in the class of '58 is a bitter disappointment to him. Denied admission to his college of choice, Yale, because it had already accepted its quota of Jews (16), Jason must settle for Harvard— and for exacting his revenge on the playing fields.

Despite his status, Jason soon realizes that, like Ted, he, too, resides on the periphery of the "real" Harvard. Raised nominally in the Unitarian Church but professing no great faith in anything but the American ethic of success and achievement, Jason is stunned, for instance, when he is passed over for membership in one of Harvard's elite Final Clubs because he is Jewish (91–95). The world's insistence that Jason embrace his Jewishness prompts him first to resentment of its judgment and then to confusion about his identity. The need to resolve his inner conflict will eventually lead Jason to Israel, where he will learn the lessons of his faith.

Daniel Rossi, *The Class*'s musical prodigy, owes a measure of his success to Jason Gilbert. On the verge of failing the infamous Harvard Step Test, completion of which will exempt him from a gym course, Danny is inspired by Jason's encouraging words and supporting gestures to fulfill this physical requirement for his degree. In doing so, he salvages additional time and energy for practice on his beloved piano, the driving passion of his life.

Danny's star rises quickly at Harvard, propelling him to the heights of fame and fortune, yet success does not bring him that which he most desires. As the epigraph by Emerson suggests, possession of the songbird does not guarantee possession of the song, for something is always missing from the original experience (6)—or in Danny's case, from his dream. All his life, Danny's "single, desperate ambition" had been "to please his father," and he had struggled valiantly to do so in the face of his conviction "that he never could" (6). Although Danny had eventually ceased trying, his need for the approval of others does not diminish. If he cannot win his father's regard, he can at least earn the public's adulation, and is willing to pay any price for it. As R. Z. Sheppard observes, he even "squanders his gifts to feed an addiction for applause" (80).

Perhaps the most brilliant of *The Class*'s major characters is the Hungarian refugee known as George Keller. When he comes to Harvard in the aftermath of the unsuccessful revolt against Soviet communism in his native land, the student who had been Gyuri Kolozsdi knows only a few words and phrases of English. George is, however, a quick study, and he has soon mastered not only the language but also the power structure of his adopted country. The protégé of Zbigniew Brzezinski and Henry Kissinger (two of the real celebrities who people the novel), George pursues a political career with ruthless determination and great success. When Kissinger is appointed National Security Adviser to Richard Nixon, George soon finds himself installed in the basement of the White House, his mentor's most valued foreign policy strategist (327). Yet in spite of his success, George, like Danny, must pay a personal price. Tormented by the ghost of Gyuri Kolozsdi, George will confront the past he felt sure he had escaped and discover its tenacious hold on the present. That confrontation, as the epigraph from "Bereft," by the American poet Robert Frost, class of 1901, suggests, will be made more difficult because George is "in my life alone," with "no one left but God" (113).

Each of these characters, as the publisher notes in what serves as a preface to the novel, "[illustrates] some of the divergent directions taken by young men of this generation into the fields of politics, the arts, intellectual life, or in voyages of self-discovery" (n.p.). Their stories of success and failure give meaning to *The Class*.

GENERIC CONVENTIONS

In developing his characters' stories, Segal creates what is essentially a *bildungsroman*, or novel of formation. The term, derived from the German author Goethe's novel *Wilhelm Meister's Apprenticeship*, denotes a literary form that deals with the development of a young person, usually from adolescence to maturity. Such novels are frequently autobiographical. According to Martin Swales, the *bildungsroman* "is a novel form that is animated by a concern for the whole man unfolding organically in all his complexity and richness" (14). The classic conception of *bildung* stresses the process by which the hero realizes the physical, intellectual, emotional, moral, and spiritual capacities inherent in his personality. Each stage of the hero's life has its own intrinsic value, but it also serves as the basis for a higher stage of development. Obstacles serve as necessary growth points through which the hero must pass on his journey to maturity. Ultimately, the purpose of that journey is to prepare the hero to accept a responsible role in a friendly social community. *The Class* deviates slightly from the generic conventions, particularly in its focus on multiple characters. In its broadest outlines and thematic purpose, however, it is indeed a novel of formation.

The Class may also be compared to a number of other contemporary "college" novels, perhaps the most famous of which is Mary McCarthy's 1963 best-seller *The Group*. A chronicle of the lives of eight Vassar coeds of the class of 1933, *The Group* is as much social history as coming-of-age story, its focus being the contemporary ideas and social mores that shaped those lives (Gelderman 245–65). Its treatment of its characters is essentially comic, unlike Segal's sober and sympathetic characterizations. Yet in their detailed depiction of the college experience and its aftermath, both *The Group* and *The Class* share common ground. Other novels that explore the old school ties include Alice Adams's *Superior Women*, Rona

Jaffe's *Class Reunion*, and Anton Myrer's *The Last Convertible*. As Susan Isaacs observes, "The popularity of these novels is fueled by the same energy that propels people to cafeterias, gymnasiums and hotel ballrooms for high school and college reunions" (9). The desire to relive golden memories and "whatever became of?", in other words, lies behind the genre.

NARRATIVE STRATEGIES: EPISODIC STRUCTURE, TIME, AND EPIGRAPHS

Episodic Structure

As a novel of formation, *The Class* is essentially episodic in structure, a series of incidents, each episode following the other in no particular order. This aspect of the narrative results at least in part from Segal's decision to chronicle several lives rather than one life. It is virtually impossible to weave together twenty-nine years in the lives of five disparate characters, all of whom have in common only their Harvard experience. In fact, several of the characters do not even know one another, thereby eliminating any possibility of integrating their experiences.

While nothing is inherently wrong with an episodic plot, in *The Class* it tends to create disjunctions in the stories of individual characters that diminish their emotional impact. The compelling story of Jason Gilbert's service in one of Israel's elite antiterrorist units, for instance, extends over thirteen years and two hundred pages and begins and ends at least six different times. The interruptions may create and enhance the story's suspense, but they also tend to sever the reader's engagement with Jason's personal struggle to define himself. Just when it seems that Jason has bested his haunted past and is ready to settle into life on the kibbutz with his wife and children, his story is interrupted by George Keller's entrapment by Soviet officials and Ted Lambros's bittersweet ascent to a coveted chair in Harvard's classics department. These stories are every bit as intriguing as Jason's story, but their impact is diminished by similar interruptions.

In her review of *The Class*, Isaacs notes several other qualities of the narrative. She observes, for instance, that for all its length it "reads more like an incredibly detailed outline than a work of fiction" and complains that Segal's prose lacks "texture," that too often summary substitutes for description and development (9). These aspects of the narrative may reflect Segal's experience as a screenwriter, for they are clearly cinematic in nature. A screenplay is little more than a plot and dialogue. Actors and sets provide the required "texture," investing characters and scenes with the specificity of real life, which the camera records. Transitions from scene to scene are marked by fade-ins and fade-outs, empty space between sequences. The viewer provides the necessary connectives. In many ways, *The Class*'s narrative is, then, like a screenplay. Segal does indeed summarize plot elements and telegraph characterization in pithy phrases and even clichés. He also uses white space as he would a fade-out, to signal movement from one episode to the next.

The problems inherent in several of *The Class*'s narrative features are tempered by Segal's use of Andrew Eliot as the connective link between the characters. As undergraduates, George Keller may never have met Danny Rossi, but both men knew Andrew, and so, too, did Ted and Jason. Even into adulthood, Andrew maintains his friendships with his classmates, and thus he is able to convey crucial information about each without stretching the novel's credibility (too much). No matter how the strands of their various lives unravel, they are inevitably stitched together by "the eternal mediator, Andrew Eliot" (175). When, for instance, Jason visits the United States after a ten-year absence, he meets Andrew at New York's Harvard Club (401), and when his marriage falls victim to his adultery and ambition, Ted telephones to commiserate with his friend (387).

Time

To handle the problems that arise from the novel's twenty-nine-year time span, Segal relies on several different plot devices, strategies for developing and controlling the elements of the story. Perhaps the most effective is the inclusion of his characters, where appropriate, in actual historical events. A member of the Israeli army, Jason sees action in the Six-Day War of 1967 (317–21), for example, and participates in the raid on Entebbe to free Jewish hostages taken in a skyjacking (460–70). Similarly, George Keller, who works on the National Security Council and nearly rises to become secretary of state, helps to effect the smooth transfer of power from Richard Nixon to Gerald Ford in the aftermath of Watergate (432–38). Even Andrew, a Wall Street banker, makes his mark on history's time line, organizing a protest against the Vietnam War by his colleagues in the financial community on "Moratorium Day" (367–

69). While the characters' involvement in these historical events underscores the range of interests and achievements of the class of '58, the
events themselves serve to mark the passing of real time in the novel's
fictional world.

Segal also uses several strategies to telescope the passing of time. He
periodically inserts the "published" announcements of significant events
in the lives of his characters. Readers know, for instance, that Ted's years
of graduate schooling are completed when they, like any other member
of the class of '58, see the paragraph in the *Harvard Alumni Bulletin* announcing the granting of his doctorate and the publication of his book
(251). Similarly, they learn of Danny's marriage and George's divorce
when Segal inserts announcements of the events that were "printed" in
Time magazine's "Milestones" column (237; 511). Use of this strategy
relieves Segal of the necessity of dramatizing every event and thereby
helps to condense fictional time. So, too, does his use of Andrew Eliot's
diary.

Like his distinguished Eliot forebears, Andrew is an inveterate diarist,
recording the "milestones" of his own life and his reactions to historical
events in the pages of personal notebooks. By inserting entries from Andrew's diary throughout *The Class*, Segal conveys the passing of time
with a minimum of explanation and dramatization. Historical events,
such as John Kennedy's assassination, are the subject of Andrew's reflections (260), but events in his own life and in the lives of his classmates
garner even more attention. The effect is to move the plot quickly
through time and to keep its focus on the characters.

Use of Andrew's diary serves yet another purpose. It reveals his character as few of the novel's scenes do. The very fact that Andrew keeps
a diary speaks especially to his self-effacing nature. Unlike Danny and
George, who chase public and professional accolades, Andrew settles for
ordinary life, convinced that he deserves nothing more. As he observes
in the diary entry with which the novel opens, "I've observed history
around me, even if I didn't make any of it" (2). He is instead *The Class*'s
Boswell. Like the eighteenth-century biographer of the English author
Samuel Johnson, Andrew records the conversations and activities of his
famous classmates. In doing so, however, he reveals much about himself.
When he records the pathos of his failed marriage and the disappointment of his strained relationship with his children, Andrew exposes the
sensitivity that makes him such a good friend. He exposes as well his
unhappiness with his own sense of failure. However modest his dreams

may have been, Andrew, like his classmates, had expected more from life.

Epigraphs

Segal relies on one other literary device, the epigraph, in *The Class*. Set at the beginning of a literary work or a division of it, the epigraph is a quotation intended to suggest the author's point. Segal uses the epigraphs in *The Class* to suggest aspects of character, as noted earlier, and to convey theme. The epigraphs also underscore the exceptional quality of Harvard students and, indeed, of Harvard itself, for all are quotations from distinguished Harvard men of letters.

The Class begins with a quotation by the psychologist and philosopher William James, who was both a graduate of and a professor at Harvard. A hymn of praise to his alma mater, the epigraph sets the tone for the novel, announcing that as "son[s] of Harvard" its characters are both fortunate and privileged. The first section of the novel, subtitled "College Years," lovingly details the truth of James's observation in its relatively uncritical depiction of the undergraduate experience.

The epigraph with which this section begins, several stanzas of a poem by John Updike, class of 1954, provides some reason for this lack of criticism as well as a general statement about these undergraduates. They "took the world as given," accepting without question the facts of their existence. Preoccupied with the "private life"—their own—they *did not know we were a generation.*" They did not understand, in other words, that their individual experiences actually comprised a common one that would unite them for life. In their self-absorption and naivete, undergraduates live the promise of their college years.

The remaining two sections of *The Class* begin with lines of poetry from *Four Quartets* by T. S. Eliot, class of 1910. The epigraph of the vast middle section, subtitled "Real Life," Segal draws from "Burnt Norton." The brief passage foreshadows the truth about "real life" that these classmates, who are now Harvard graduates, will soon learn. Their idyllic college years behind them, they must now face the challenges of adulthood—marriage, parenthood, career—in a world that is far less hospitable than Harvard's sheltered quads. They are about to learn that real life, as Eliot's phrase indicates, is more than human beings can sometimes bear (195).

The epigraph of the final section of *The Class*, subtitled "The Reunion," is a passage from Eliot's poem "Little Gidding" that suggests the nature of the twenty-five-year journey that the class of '58 has taken. Whereas their undergraduate selves had arrived at Harvard oblivious to others and even to their own part in some larger drama, their adult selves return to Harvard capable of understanding its meaning. The measure of their growth and maturity is, in fact, their ability to return to their point of departure and to "know the place for the first time" (513). Their twenty-fifth-year class reunion is now beginning from their original point of departure, but with a whole new view of the journey that was and the journey to come.

THEMATIC DEVELOPMENT

The epigraphs with which each segment of the novel begins, like its generic conventions, ultimately reinforce Segal's thematic preoccupations in *The Class*. In the novel of formation, the protagonist journeys from innocence to experience, from ignorance to enlightenment, and such is the case for Segal's classmates. By novel's end they have learned important lessons about life and about self, as the epigraphs suggest. Their youthful enthusiasm has been tempered by a knowledge of limitation and an understanding of the toll exacted by life. Indeed, their journeys challenge them to reevaluate their dreams and revise their notions of success. Thus, the characters' lives and experiences give shape to the thematic core of *The Class*.

In Jason Gilbert's story, Segal focuses on the quest for identity and its importance to personal happiness and fulfillment. Until he entered Harvard, Jason felt certain of both his identity and his destiny—he was an American destined for success. Everything in his background supported his belief, everything except his Jewish heritage. Until he entered Harvard, Jason was not Jewish. This belief was not a matter of denial, but rather of an upbringing by thoroughly assimilated Jewish parents. At Harvard, however, Jason finds his Jewishness foisted upon him. As a freshman, he is assigned a Jewish roommate (43). As a sophomore, he is denied membership in the prestigious Final Clubs because he is Jewish (91–95). By the time he is a junior, he is so confused about his identity that he is taking his first tentative steps toward his religious heritage. Accompanied by a tennis teammate, he attends his first Passover seder and leaves convinced of his friend's good fortune. "He's got an identity" (153), Jason silently acknowledges.

Real life brings Jason to resolution of his doubts. When his fiancée is killed in a terrorist attack on a kibbutz, Jason travels to Israel and unexpectedly finds home. Intent on avenging Fanny's death, Jason abandons law school and stays on at the kibbutz, where he learns gradually to embrace his Jewishness. His commitment to Israel is sealed when he joins the army and fights to join its elite antiterrorist unit. Through marriage and parenthood, nothing can shake his allegiance to his faith and to the future of his adopted home, and he will die in the raid on Entebbe to preserve this part of himself. Jason's life and death are a triumph over uncertainty. In resolving his questions about his identity, Jason finds the peace that passes all understanding, the fulfillment of his life's dream. His other classmates, Jason's story asserts, should be so blessed.

In this novel of development, all of the characters will struggle to some degree with the problem of self-definition. Andrew Eliot, for instance, who bears the burden of family expectations, is so convinced that he will "remain a caterpillar all [his] life" (59) that he is not quite sure that he "really want[s] to grow up" (41). And Ted Lambros, "the son of an insecure immigrant" (18), makes a Harvard professorship his goal in part because he admires and desires the self-confidence such men possess, "their ability to love themselves and treasure their own intellects" (18). The question of self-definition for Jason's classmates, however, is subsumed in Segal's exploration of the nature of success, *The Class*'s central theme.

Segal's development of this theme is primarily a matter of contrasting public and professional with private and personal definitions of success. Three of the novel's protagonists pursue with a vengeance professional recognition, public acclaim, some sort of external validation of their abilities and achievements. The price of success for these men is personal— failed marriages, physical and psychological deterioration. Their fates are Segal's statement on the subject.

Ted Lambros, *The Class*'s brilliant but insecure academic, invests his whole sense of self in pursuit of a Harvard professorship. To attain such a position will validate him professionally, but more important, it will signify full acceptance into a community that has always seemed closed to a man who defines himself as a perpetual "townie." Because nothing but a Harvard professorship will do, Ted is devastated when he fails to achieve tenure. Ignoring the advice of his colleagues and his wife, who urge him to accept an equally prestigious position in California, Ted settles for a professorship at a small private college in New England, unable to cut his ties to Harvard's hallowed halls.

Ted will eventually attain his goal. In fact, by his twenty-fifth-year class reunion, he will have risen to become dean of his alma mater. His success, however, will cost him his wife Sara. His college sweetheart, Sara had supported her husband's fragile ego throughout their courtship and marriage. She had sacrificed her own intellect to his, had followed him willingly to exile at Canterbury College. But Sara will not forgive Ted's adultery. His brief and meaningless affair with a student during his sabbatical at Oxford is a betrayal of Sara's love and trust. Too late, Ted understands what he has done. Too late, he understands what he has lost. Years later, at the moment of his triumph, Ted will confess to Sara, "I'd give up anything—including Harvard—if we could still be together" (458). Too late, Ted regrets his sacrifice of love for acceptance.

Danny Rossi, *The Class*'s musical genius, nearly pays the same price as Ted for his fame and fortune. Unable to resist the women who are unable to resist his talents, Danny engages in an endless series of meaningless affairs that almost destroy his marriage. Driven by the applause that confirms his own sense of greatness, Danny nearly squanders his talent in restless pursuit of yet another concert performance, yet another recording contract, yet another conducting opportunity in venues around the world. To Segal, Danny's early success merely "protracted his adolescence" (Smith 45). Only religious scruples prevent his wife Maria from divorcing a man who had always had to have everything *now*.

The frenetic pace of Danny's life eventually takes its toll. Physically exhausted, Danny finds a doctor who will prescribe what he needs to "feel good." Before long, he is dependent on a potent combination of drugs to sleep, to awake, to perform, to live. Those drugs, however, sabotage Danny's career. When he develops a neurological disorder that causes uncontrollable shaking in his hands, Danny's career as a concert pianist, his area of real genius, is ended. He had settled for youthful genius rather than mature talent. He had traded fleeting fame for lasting influence.

In his rise to the heights of political power, George Keller leaves behind everyone he had ever loved, including himself. When he flees Communist Hungary, George abandons his sister, his father, and the woman who loved him. In fact, when she is gunned down by a border patrol during their daring escape, George fails at first to notice and then makes no effort to locate and assist her. Because he must save himself, it is expedient for him to assume that she has been killed. Expediency eventually becomes the guiding principle of George's life. The first words he masters in English are "cool cat," compliments intended "to flatter his future countrymen" (131). At Harvard, he transfers his loyalties from Brzezinski, his patron, to Kissinger, a man on the move. In Washington, he pays his debt to his mentor with betrayal and allows his marriage to wither of neglect.

Buried inside George Keller, however, is Gyuri Kolozsdi, the self he had been, and a brief visit to his homeland at his father's death forces him to confront that self and to evaluate his past. The reckoning will push George to suicide. In many ways, George was still the small, lonely, sad boy who loved and hated his father, who grieved for the mother who had loved him. Knowing and expecting nothing but loss, George was unable to accept love and thus condemned himself to an empty existence that was ultimately more than he could bear. He may have earned burial in Arlington Cemetery, but as Cathy, his ex-wife, tells Andrew, "the price was too high" (531). Success could simply not erase the pain of the past or compensate for the unhappiness of the present. Commenting on his connection to George, Segal states, "He's all the values I reject but that are still part of me" (Smith 45).

Not surprisingly, given his self-defeating attitudes, Andrew Eliot, the one man who values marriage and parenthood and who measures his success in such personal terms, fails at both, but certainly not for trying. Andrew's unremarkable efforts to live a good life, however, and to be a good person are ultimately remarkable. As chair of the reunion fundraising drive, Andrew earns special and unexpected recognition from his alma mater. The honor brings him pleasure and pride, especially because his daughter is present to share the moment with him.

In this moment of quiet triumph at the novel's end lies the meaning of success in *The Class*. At their class reunion, all of the central characters know the meaning of compromise (515) and "the terror of *insignificance*. Of not being remembered, not counting" (517). Their "unbounded faith in their potential" (515) has been tempered by the experience of real life, and they now understand that public and professional glory commands high premiums but is no guarantee of happiness and fulfillment. In fact, this is the lesson that the lives of Segal's classmates now teach.

A MARXIST READING OF *THE CLASS*

The novel's title, *The Class*, and its depiction of its rather closed society suggest one alternative perspective from which to evaluate it, especially for the Marxist critic. Such a critic focuses on the relation between literature and history, emphasizing particularly the social and economic factors that, according to the philosopher Karl Marx (1818–1883), drive historical change. Like feminism, with which it shares some basic tenets, Marxism is not a single theory. In fact, several different schools of Marxist critics exist, and "all of them," according to Arthur Asa Berger, "base their criticism on varying and sometimes conflicting interpretations of Marx's theories and how they can be applied to analyzing culture in general and, more specifically, literary texts, works of elite culture, popular culture, and the mass media" (41). To understand Marxist criticism, then, we need first to explain briefly the concepts that serve as its foundation.

Marx is usually classified as a "dialectical materialist." He believed that historical transformations occur through a dialectic, or development, through the stages of thesis, antithesis, and synthesis. Each historical force, according to Marx, calls into being its Other so that the two opposing forces negate each other and eventually give rise to a third force that transcends its opposition. Unlike his great teacher Hegel, who was an idealist, Marx was a materialist who believed that social forces shape human consciousness.

In Marxism, the ultimate moving force of human history is economics, or perhaps more specifically, political economy. This term encompasses political and social issues as well as economic factors. Each society, according to Marx, bases its culture upon its means of production, the techniques by which it produces food, clothing, shelter, and other necessities of life, and the social relations these methods create. For example, an economy based on manufacturing demands a division of labor, cooperation among workers, and a hierarchical system of managers. These economic demands in turn shape the social relations of the people. From this basic premise, Marx argued that major historical changes occur as a result of economic contradictions, what might be termed class consciousness and class conflict. The source of the French Revolution of the 1790s, for example, was conflict between the aristocracy and the middle classes.

In Marxist thought, the economic base gives rise to and shapes the superstructure, which finds expression in the culture's ideology, its collective consciousness of itself. This ideology consists of all the institutions of the society, such as the church, the education system, the art world, and the legal system. Generally, the ideology, which includes literature, conforms to and supports the culture's dominant means of production. Economic conditions alone, however, are not sufficient to explain the development and effect of its institutions. Human agency, or individual consciousness, is active in these institutions as well. Thus, Marxist criticism that focuses exclusively on economics and that celebrates the proletariat, or working class, has been termed "vulgar Marxism" for is crude tendency to oversimplify complex issues.

Marxism is primarily a political and economic philosophy, not a guide to understanding literature. As a result, Marxist criticism takes a variety of forms, depending upon how the text is defined in relation to material reality or to ideology. Segal's presentation of the closed world of Harvard University lends itself most readily to a Marxist critique based upon the reflection theory. As an imitation of the culture that helped to produce it, *The Class* reveals the social, political, and economic forces that uphold this privileged world—significant aspects of which are class consciousness and class conflict.

On the surface, Segal's depiction of Harvard and its institutions and traditions is lovingly rendered and positive in tone. From registration at Memorial Hall and the selection of the requisite green bookbag at The Coop (30) to dinner at the Freshman Union (30–31) and the celebrated lectures of Professor Finley in Sanders Theater, Segal records the unique details of the Harvard experience. In so doing, he makes Harvard the novel's sixth character, with a life and purpose—to teach its students lessons in limitations (48)—all its own. Segal's attitude toward this character, which imparts the novel's tone, is one of fond regard for an old friend.

That regard, however, is tempered by a knowing and subtle criticism of the Harvard world. In its institutions and its traditions, Harvard is a closed society, requiring a ticket of admission from everyone who is privileged to teach and to learn in its environs. It is also a microcosm, a little world that duplicates and reflects its larger counterpart. Not surprisingly, then, the world of Harvard is rife with racism, sexism, elitism. Class consciousness is the very foundation of its existence.

Ted Lambros, for instance, is utterly correct in his feelings of exclusion from the "real" Harvard, for a deeply entrenched "old boy" network dominates the university. Ted may be a brilliant scholar and an inspiring teacher, but achieving tenure at Harvard is as much about acceptance, about fitting in, as it is about merit. It is as much about background and breeding and reputation as it is about talent. So a man of proven ability like Ted, who was never part of the "Harris Tweed underground" (40), is at a disadvantage against the Mike Wigglesworths and Dickie Newalls and even the Andrew Eliots of the Harvard world. They may have none of the talent or intelligence of Ted, but they are members of the club—the right club. Their "preppie" backgrounds virtually guarantee their places in the world.

Racism and sexism are also among "the not-so-commendable facts of Harvard life" (92). Jason Gilbert, of course, falls victim to their ugly reality, but the presence of two other characters, Tod Anderson and Sara Lambros, provides further evidence of their pervasiveness. Anderson, a popular athlete, is denied admission to Harvard's Hasty Pudding Club, the eating society to which nearly a third of all upperclassmen belong, because he is African American. When Jason expresses disbelief about Tod's exclusion, Dickie chides him for his naivete: "Come on, Gilbert, the Pudding's not *that* liberal. I mean, we've still got to keep *somebody* out" (144).

Sara Lambros, Ted's wife, is every bit the intellectual equal of her husband, but when she graduates with honors from Radcliffe, Harvard's sister school, her sex limits her opportunities. She dutifully follows the expected career path of marriage and motherhood and even takes a secretarial course to acquire the skills that will earn her an entry-level position at Harvard University Press, where she will gain inside information that may help to advance her husband's career. Although she asks for and receives no credit for intellectual contributions to Ted's academic achievements, Sara is his invisible collaborator. Divorce and changing times will eventually give Sara the opportunity to earn her own advanced degree and even to become her ex-husband's principal rival for a coveted position in the Harvard classics department. But at the Harvard of her undergraduate days, Sara would have been denied admission strictly on the basis of her sex alone.

Change comes with the times at Harvard, but it comes slowly. By the time of the twenty-fifth-year reunion, Ted Lambros, the perpetual outsider, is dean of the university, and Tod Anderson is assistant dean of admissions to Harvard Law School (460). Yet the fact that change comes slowly to a symbol of enlightenment such as Harvard is disconcerting. So, too, is the fact that some of its changes may have resulted from federal equal opportunity mandates. All things being equal, for instance, Sara vaults over Ted to the top of the candidacy list for the classics chair because she is a woman (456). In the end, readers are left to wonder if the best and the brightest really do get the opportunity to succeed or if the invisible barriers of class forever block the way. After all, Andrew's daughter Lizzie seems destined to be next in the long line of Eliots to walk through Harvard's gates (519).

Class, however, is not the primary focus of *The Class*. What persists in the end are the stories of five young men, representative in some ways, who make the journey from innocence to experience, from the naive good faith to the tragic awareness of limitation that is called growing up. Theirs are the stories of generations.

7

Doctors
(1988)

In one of the epigraphs to his fifth best-seller, *Doctors* (1988), Erich Segal "quotes" one of the novel's central characters, Barney Livingston, M.D., to announce his central focus. A psychiatrist, Livingston asserts, "We have turned doctors into gods and worship their deity by offering up our bodies and our souls. And yet paradoxically, they are the most vulnerable of human beings." In his saga of four men and women who sacrifice nearly everything to the practice of medicine, Segal illustrates the truth of Livingston's diagnosis. As they struggle to balance their personal and professional lives, Segal's doctors learn valuable lessons about their powers of endurance and their strength of character while facing the truth of their human fallibility. Their struggles and challenges expose the awesome truth about the healers who seemingly hold in their hands the power of life and death.

A novel that ranges through more than thirty years of social and political change and medical and scientific discovery, *Doctors* explores the lives of Harvard Medical School's class of 1962, focusing particularly upon the experiences of three men and one woman who are typical even in their atypicality. Segal chronicles the gruelling medical training that transforms them into doctors and the equally demanding requirements of internship and residency that certify their competency, capturing the harrowing reality of the experience. He also reveals the inner lives of those who pursue a career in medicine, exposing the personal motives—

the doubts, fears, hurts, ambitions—that lie behind their decisions and actions. As much as anything, however, *Doctors* is a love story about childhood friends, Barney Livingston and Laura Castellano, whose shared history and aspirations ultimately are the seeds of passion. From such disparate elements does Segal construct *Doctors*.

CHARACTERIZATION

At the heart of *Doctors* are the men and women who struggle daily against accident, sickness, disease, and their own human failings in order to heal their fellow sufferers. The novel's characters have lives and histories uniquely their own, and Segal interweaves their individual stories to give shape to his plot. Segal's doctors are also, however, representative. Two are white men, the traditional healers of the sick and infirm and members of the medical elite. Two—an African-American male and a woman—are minority representatives, reluctantly admitted, but not fully accepted into a tradition-bound, hierarchical profession. All four will find medical school a challenge to their senses of self and to their deepest-held beliefs about others. Like *The Class*, then, its immediate predecessor, *Doctors* is essentially a *bildungsroman*, or novel of development, a literary genre more fully explained in the preceding chapter. Character development gives focus to its plot.

Childhood friends Barney Livingston and Laura Castellano are the novel's primary characters, and their first meeting serves as a paradigm for both their individual selves and their mutual relationship. The new child on the block, Laura is initially a disappointment to her next-door neighbor Barney, for she is, after all, a girl. Five-year-old Laura, however, is unlike any girl he has ever known. Capable of vaulting with ease the fence separating their yards, she also plays a fair game of catch, and she knows all about the rituals of doctoring. In fact, at their first meeting, she suggests that they strip and take turns "esamining" each other as doctor and patient (5–6). Their game of pretend is, of course, prophetic, foreshadowing the professional path both will travel. Both will also spend much of their lives analyzing themselves and each other as they struggle for self-knowledge, building love on the foundation of friendship.

Laura is indeed an exceptional girl and woman. Bright, articulate, competent, and beautiful, she is also extremely ambitious. Traditional barriers do not deter Laura from pursuing her goals. Instead, they are challenges to surmount, thereby proving her ability to others. When she makes the unprecedented decision, for instance, to run for class president, she does so for a strictly "selfish" reason—she thinks it is "the surest way of getting into a good college" (45), a necessity if she hopes to have any chance of being among the handful of women who are accepted to medical school.

Yet for all her determination to succeed, Laura is plagued by doubts and insecurities that seriously undermine her self-esteem. When her younger sister, Isobel, dies of polio, Laura is burdened by guilt about her survival, and her parents' intense grief fuels her anxiety. As her mother withdraws into religion and her father into liquor, Laura feels herself abandoned and unloved (23). Childhood for Laura ends with Isobel's death, for the knowledge that the fact of her existence is insufficient to her parents robs her of the security that nurtures self-esteem. Even into adulthood, Laura will suffer the pain of this knowledge. When, as a student in medical school, she discovers a cache of poetry written by her father to his unborn son, Laura is devastated by the proof of her own insignificance. Only Barney's understanding and support give her the strength to move forward in life (282–83).

Laura's marriage to Palmer Talbot and her affair with Marshall Jaffe—indeed, her sexual relationship with any of the men in her life—offer further proof of her lack of self-worth. The daughter of refugees from the Spanish Civil War, Laura has inherited the blonde beauty of her Celtic ancestors (19). That beauty, however, is more a curse than a blessing because it causes Laura to doubt the feelings of the men in her life. Although Palmer genuinely loves her and even defers a marriage that he eagerly desires until she completes medical school, Laura is uncertain of the depth of her own feelings for him, primarily because she doubts that any man can love her for her self and not her beauty. Because she never really commits to the relationship, Palmer eventually does betray her, thereby confirming her deepest fears. Laura's marriage to Palmer is the paradigm for her relationship with other men—everyone, that is, except Barney.

A man born to become a psychiatrist, Barney combines athletic prowess on the basketball court with compassion for and sensitivity to the feelings of others. First Laura and then his other medical school classmates make Barney their confidant, seeking his counsel because they recognize his ability to empathize with their suffering and confusion. Barney, however, rather ironically possesses the ability to analyze the lives and needs of others but not his own. In fact, he will eventually acknowledge that his desire to be "the man dispensing wisdom" is a form of "self-protection" (310), that he both fears and needs to know what he might discover if he looks within himself.

Like Laura, Barney, too, grows to maturity believing that he has failed his father. Harold Livingston had been serving in World War II during Barney's early childhood, and during his absence, Luis Castellano, a "rugged bearlike physician" (12) had become not only a substitute father but also a role model to Barney. When Harold, a scholarly Latin teacher, returns from the war a shadow of his former self, Barney's disappointment is almost palpable. More concerned with nursing his own psychic wounds than in nurturing his son, Harold prefers the isolation of his study and the comfort of his books to shooting hoops with his son or even cheering his performance on the court. When permanent disability forces his father into early retirement, Barney sacrifices the one activity that brings him any self-affirmation—playing basketball—to the family's need for supplemental income and takes a job in a local pharmacy. Barney and his father eventually find common ground in their love of learning and their interest in psychology, and although Barney will be genuinely saddened by his death, only once in his life will he feel the glow of his father's approval (29). For Barney, once is simply not enough.

Between Laura and Barney is an intuitive understanding of the other's thoughts and feelings (18). Each is the other's closest friend and chief confidant, and they are united by bonds of absolute trust. In Barney only has Laura confided her feelings of rejection and betrayal. To Barney only has she revealed her own shortcomings and failures as a person. He is her friend, she knows, because he understands and accepts her as she is. Similarly, only Laura recognizes Barney's own feelings of rejection by a distant father. Only Laura sympathizes with his profound disappointment in the relationship. Their own relationship, then, takes root in their shared history and common dream of becoming doctors (19). It is the one constant in both their lives. Eventually, they will also acknowledge the sexual attraction that has always lain dormant between them. In fact, neither finds happiness in a marriage partner until they admit that what they seek in a husband or wife is each other. Together, they finally know the "indescribable feeling of wholeness" (595).

When Laura and Barney begin their studies at Harvard Medical School, Segal introduces the other players in his novel. Bennett Landsmann, for example, is both an anomaly among and an "enigma" (128) to his classmates. A collegiate basketball star, Landsmann is a handsome, articulate, cultured, charismatic African American, the sole representative of his race in the class of 1962. Intensely private, he stands seemingly aloof from his classmates, but Barney's ability to penetrate defenses, whether on the basketball court or in life, gradually exposes the raw edges of Bennett's past.

Bennett's father, Colonel Abraham Lincoln Bennett, had been in command of the troops that liberated some of Nazi Germany's most notorious death camps in 1945, and among those who owed their lives to him and his troops were Herschel and Hannah Landsmann. When Colonel Bennett dies of typhus contracted in those death camps, the Landsmanns vow to dedicate their lives to his only child. Following their emigration to the United States, they locate Colonel Bennett's son, who lives in relative poverty with his grandmother in a segregated Georgia town, and offer him opportunities and a life with them in an affluent Cleveland suburb. Linc Junior reluctantly accepts their offer and grows to maturity in the supportive environment of his Jewish home. In adolescence he even supports the Landsmanns' wish to adopt him, thereby recreating himself as Bennett Landsmann, the child of two families.

Self-definition, however, is not solely a matter of personal choice. Bennett may share his life with people who are paragons of tolerance and inclusivity, but beyond the haven of home lies a world where race, religion, and ethnicity are important criteria for judging individual worth and determining membership in the group. As a black Jew, Bennett is "caught in no-man's-land between two separate and distinct societies" (330), neither of which claims him as its own and in neither of which does he feel comfortable. Daily some subtle reminder or overt incident makes him feel his "otherness" (330).

Confused about his identity, Bennett attempts to define himself professionally, as a surgeon. He finds his efforts thwarted, however, by the turbulence of the times. The period of his surgical residency coincides with that of the Civil Rights movement, and members of the African-American community pressure him to join the cause of his race, even if it essentially demands that he repudiate his parents. While Bennett stands on principle and rebuffs such assaults on his allegiances, he is powerless against a cruel and ironic twist of fate that strips him of his identity. Rushing to the aid of a man who is choking to death in a restaurant, Bennett is performing emergency surgery with a steak knife when the police arrive. Seeing a black man, not a surgeon, holding a knife on a white man, the police brutally beat Bennett. His injuries end his promising career and force him to reinvent himself once again, but with no more success. To the end, Bennett lives both personally and professionally on the periphery.

Seth Lazarus, the fourth of the major characters in *Doctors*, graduates at the top of the class of 1962, yet few would have thought that his brilliance would lead to notoriety. Painfully shy, he buries himself in books or in the laboratory. Acutely sensitive to suffering, he cannot bear to prolong the dying of the terminally ill or the incurable, for he knows its destructive power. As a toddler, Seth's older brother, Howie, had been grievously injured in an automobile accident. He had then spent the next twenty-five years of his life hospitalized in a vegetative state, sustained at times by feeding tubes, breathing apparatus, and miracle drugs. Howie's "life" was a torture to him, but it exacted an equally painful toll on the other Lazarus family members, all of whom felt guilty for their existence and so took little pleasure from it.

Howie's condition leads Seth to a deeply held belief in the doctor's responsibility to end the pain and suffering of those for whom medicine can do nothing. Unlike the biblical Lazarus, in other words, who Jesus raised from the dead, this Lazarus puts others to death. When Howie, for example, suffers a cerebral hemorrhage and is once again placed on life-support systems, Seth administers a lethal injection to end his brother's dying. He will take similar action on at least four other occasions before his treatment is exposed and he finds himself at the center of medical and legal controversy. As the notorious "Doctor Death," the ironically named Seth Lazarus then calls upon a classmate and forensic specialist, Bennett Landsmann, to defend him in a case that asks everyone to consider the meaning of life and existence.

Despite the novel's breadth, its characters do not have much depth or complexity. All of the major characters study medicine in what amounts to an attempt to cure themselves, to relieve their own hurt and suffering. They all know the pain of guilt and the ache of desire. They all long for self-affirming parental approval, or even notice. While self-analysis may not be inherent in the study of medicine, it is certainly so in *Doctors*. Yet for all their efforts to know themselves, Segal's characters grow and change very little during the course of their fictional lives. Their natures are so constituted to be nearly fixed from their first appearance in the novel.

If Segal's major characters are rather one-dimensional, his minor characters are even more so. Lance Mortimer, Hank Dwyer, and Grete Anderson, three other members of the class of 1962, are little more than stereotypes. Lance, for instance, chooses anesthesiology as a speciality not because it provides him with an opportunity to serve but because it commands the highest salary for the least effort and responsibility. He is the doctor as crass materialist. Hank Dwyer, a failed priest, forsakes the soul for the body—of every available nurse. The father of six children by two different women, one of whom is a prostitute he "marries" during a voluntary tour of duty in the Vietnam War, Hank eventually opens a fertility clinic in Hawaii. He is a parody, or comic imitation, of the doctor as God the Creator. Within the novel, characters such as these advance thematic concerns or help to expose the qualities of the major characters. In other words, they are functional rather than integral characters.

NARRATIVE STRATEGIES: TIME, STRUCTURE, AND EPIGRAPHS

Time

Like *The Class*, *Doctors* ranges across nearly forty years of historical, social, and political change, and Segal uses that background to give focus and shape to his narrative as well as enhance its surface realism. It also provides a context for character development and thematic ideas. The revolutionary politics of the Spanish Civil War, for example, shape the life of Luis Castellano, forcing him first to seek refuge in the United States and prompting him later to join Che Guevara and Fidel Castro in Cuba. In fact, his decision to support these guerilla leaders makes sense only within the context of his own commitment to social and political change and his previous involvement in revolutionary movements. Similarly, Bennett's refusal to join the Black Panthers during the 1960s must be placed within the context of the Holocaust and his Jewish parents. He will indeed support the Civil Rights movement and will even participate, as does Laura, in the March on Washington, but he will not support the radicals of the movement, who blame one group for the situation of another.

Grounding the novel in historical time also allows Segal to chart changes and advances in medicine itself. In 1946, for example, Laura's younger sister, Isobel, dies of an illness that Dr. Jonas Salk's vaccine will virtually eradicate less than ten years later—polio. The development of the birth control pill in the 1960s will usher in a new era of sexual freedom—and place strains on the marriage of Hank and Cheryl Dwyer because her devout Roman Catholicism conflicts with medical advancements. By 1978, the birth of Louise Brown, the first "test tube baby," will popularize the new reproductive technologies—and make Hank a celebrity healer. Eventually, Laura and Barney's own child will be saved from a rare and virtually incurable condition by experimental medicine. The real advances of medicine that Segal makes integral to the novel's plot do much to increase readers' awareness of and appreciation for the healing arts.

Structure

Segal also controls his narrative by dividing the plot into three distinct sections. The first section, "Innocence," begins with the meeting of Laura and Barney in 1942 and ends with their acceptance to Harvard Medical School in 1958. "Becoming Doctors," the second section, dramatizes the personal struggles and professional training of the class of 1962, focusing especially on the novel's major characters and the handful of minor figures with whom their lives connect. The third section, "Being Doctors," takes those same characters through their hospital internships and residencies as well as through the establishment of private practices and individual specializations. These plot divisions draw attention to the various stages of the characters' lives and experiences, thereby emphasizing the novel's generic form as a *bildungsroman*. Each stage of the characters' lives increases their level of maturity and commitment and brings them to a greater self-awareness. Through the various stages of their lives they are indeed building selves.

Epigraphs

One other narrative device characteristic of Segal's style also gives shape to *Doctors*. Segal begins each section of the novel with an epigraph that highlights its plot development or thematic focus, and each of the epigraphs, or opening quotations, is an observation by or about physicians. William Carlos Williams, the American poet, was a pediatrician, so his words are most appropriate to a section of the novel devoted to the childhood and young adulthood of Laura and Barney. Born into a "new world naked" in their "innocence," the frequently ironic section title, they do indeed take root and "begin to awaken." They do indeed thrive and grow, but from the time they are born, "the profound change" takes their innocence from them, bringing them to the world of inescapable fact to which Oliver Wendell Holmes refers in the epigraph to the novel's second section.

Holmes, a professor of anatomy and a dean of the Harvard Medical School in the nineteenth century, speaks with disdain of the "horror" of facts, calling them the "brute beasts of the intellectual domain." Members of the class of 1962, who will find themselves bullied and confounded by the facts of medicine, will experience the truth of Holmes's observation. As they reduce the mysteries of the body to chemical compounds and organic function and the vagaries of disease and sickness to symptoms and treatments, those who are "becoming doctors" fear the loss of independent thought, the spark capable of transforming fact into something other than sheer information.

The epigraph to the novel's third section, a biblical passage from Ecclesiastes, commends the person who has sinned to "the hand of the Physician," confirming that healer's authority and ability to minister to the "dis-eased." Yet the lives of Segal's doctors offer testimony of another sort. Too often, in fact, his physicians are most in need of healing, but they are unable to diagnose their conditions or to prescribe appropriate treatment. They are the "wounded healers" to which the epigraph of the entire novel refers. Thus, the disjunction between the ideal, evoked in the section's epigraph, and the actual, dramatized in the novel, brings readers to *Doctors'* thematic focus.

THEMATIC DEVELOPMENT

Well into the novel, as he discusses his concept for a second book with his editor, Barney Livingston shares with him and with readers the central theme of *Doctors*: "Doctors are like every other human being" (481). Around the physician has grown a myth. He is a god, all-knowing and infallible, who holds the power of life and death. As Bill Chaplin, Barney's editor, notes, "the man in the street thinks the doctor is a priest with a hotline to God. We worship them. We're scared of them" (480). "Doctors," however, Barney contradicts, "are as far from being heros as any group I have ever known" (480). The majority are engaged in a "Sisyphan task, just hoping that the rock won't roll over them" (480), and the reality of their lives and their profession is far different from the idealized versions lived by Ben Casey and Dr. Kildare, two popular television doctors of the time. Barney intends to write the real story of doctors. He intends, in other words, to write the story that Segal has written in *Doctors*.

To demythologize the myth of the doctor as god, Segal dramatizes the personal failings of his central characters and the collective failings of representative types within the profession. He also exposes the politics of the profession. He even evokes history, by focusing on the Holocaust, to raise the specter of the doctor corrupted. The evidence confirms the truth of Barney's pronouncement.

Although a key precept of Socrates' philosophy was "Know thyself," the physician's doctrine, "Heal thyself," rings a variation on that human truth. The journey from innocence to maturity should indeed result in self-knowledge, but it may also require soothing balms for the sometimes painful truths such knowledge brings. So it is ironic that Segal's central characters, men and a woman trained to minister to the pain of others, suffer psychological wounds that they are unable to heal.

All of them, for instance, bear the scars of parental rejection. Laura lives daily with the painful knowledge that she is an orphan with two parents, and Seth is seldom honest about the feelings of neglect that resulted from his parents' attention to Howie. Just beneath the surface of Bennett's cool composure lies a fear of rejection that springs from his mother's abandonment of him as a child, yet the doctor will not admit this truth until Barney confronts him with it (632–33). None of these doctors is capable of self-healing. In fact, even Barney, the psychiatrist, cannot forget his disappointment when his father failed to attend his basketball games, and he is angry that his father died before he could prove his worthiness (405). If the doctor trained to minister to the mind struggles to achieve psychic health himself, then he or she is certainly no different from the mass of suffering humanity, who bear their own private pain and "dis-ease."

Segal's central characters are highly principled individuals who enter the field of medicine for noble motives. Another breed of doctor, however, exists. Bill Chaplin, Barney's editor, describes them as "venal, insecure schmucks in white coats who use the letters M and D as crutches to hold them up in society" (480), and Barney acknowledges the validity of his claim. Segal offers his own validation with examples from the class of 1962. Lance Mortimer, for example, chooses anesthesiology as a specialty because it affords the opportunity to earn the most money for the least work. The toast of every party in Hollywood, where he chooses to practice, Lance comes equipped with tanks of gas guaranteed to keep revelers laughing—and making a mockery of his profession (426). In their own way, Hank Dwyer, Grete Anderson, and Peter Wyman also dishonor their profession by personal conduct revealing human weaknesses that make them far from infallible.

Politics, Segal makes clear, is also rife in the medical profession. Students at Harvard Medical School are not above sabotaging their classmates' work to prevent them from earning high marks, and such cutthroat tactics persist among those who play medicine like a competitive sport. Peter Wyman, for instance, is dismissed from his postgraduate research fellowship because he not only manufactures corroboration for his theories but also promotes himself at the expense of his superiors (443–47). Laura, too, will fall victim to medical politics. Conducting research at the National Institutes of Health, she helps her colleague and lover, Marshall Jaffe, expose the director's intention to omit the names of team members from a published report of their findings, only to discover that one of those uncredited doctors had already outwitted the director by patenting the work for himself. In a world where reputations—and grant money—are at stake, nobody is immune from the disease of ambition.

Perhaps the novel's most fearsome example of the doctor's humanity is the utter inhumanity of those who perfected their skill and knowledge by experimenting on Jewish victims of the Holocaust. Bennett Landsmann's adopted mother Hannah was one of those victims. When Bennett's natural father liberated the death camp in which Hannah had been imprisoned, doctors had already pronounced her imminent death and turned their attention to others who still had a chance of survival. Used as a "human guinea pig" by Nazi doctors who were experimenting with drugs to combat venereal disease, Hannah was slowly and painfully dying of their "cure," her reproductive organs eaten away by the corrosive action of lye. Before he himself died of typhus, Bennett's father ordered Allied surgeons to perform a hysterectomy on Hannah, thereby saving her life, but she would, of course, never bear other children to take the place of a daughter sent early in the war to the crematorium (158–63).

There are other doctors in the novel who shirk their responsibilities or whose ineptness causes pain, suffering, and even death. Barney's father, for instance, dies because a doctor fearing legal ramifications should something go wrong refuses an appeal for emergency assistance, and Laura is unable to save a newborn in respiratory distress because someone failed to fill the oxygen tanks. Such failures pale in comparison, however, to the deliberate perversion of the healing arts practiced by Nazi doctors. This episode of the novel may initially seem unrelated and unnecessary to the whole, but within the context of Segal's central theme, it clearly is not.

Early in their medical schooling, Barney and Laura and the other members of the class of 1962 begin a "voyage" that "set[s] them apart from laymen whose apprehension of the awesome machinery of life was, literally, skin deep" (173). That journey does not, however, make them superior to other human beings nor does it rob them of their humanity. For all their knowledge, doctors are "painfully aware of just how little anybody understands about curing the sick" (249), among whom they are often numbered, and all too often they must camouflage their ignorance with a diagnosis of "idiopathic," meaning of unknown origin (315). Like their patients, doctors fall prey to sickness and disease and their own human failings. Like their patients, they struggle to achieve and maintain good physical and mental health and to live satisfying and fulfilling lives.

Doctors are indeed like other human beings, capable of good as well as evil, and medicine is an inexact science. This is the central theme of *Doctors*, and Segal hammers it home in the novel's final medical emergency. When Laura and Barney's only child develops a rare condition for which there is no known cure, these all-too-human doctors are willing to try anything, to seek help from anyone, to save their loved one. In California, where they take their son for an experimental treatment, Harry not only swallows Peter Wyman's drugs, but also undergoes Dr. Hsiang's acupuncture treatment and drinks his herbal medicine. Miraculously, he recovers. "What was it, [Barney] asked himself," unable to explain the miracle. "Wyman's enzyme? The Chinese potion? A doctor's trick? A parent's love?" (675). Some mysteries science cannot explain, and even those who practice the healing arts, no matter what their training, must live with the mystery, like the rest of us.

A DECONSTRUCTIONIST READING OF *DOCTORS*

While the plot, characters, and narrative strategies clearly give focus to the central theme of *Doctors* and do indeed demythologize the myth of the doctor as superior being, from another perspective, the deconstructionist's, those same elements simultaneously reconstruct the myth. A widespread philosophical and critical movement, deconstruction owes its name and energy to the precepts and examples of the French philosopher Jacques Derrida, whose works have been available in English translation since the 1960s. Derrida argues that all thought is necessarily inscribed in language and that language itself is fraught with intractable paradoxes, or self-contradictions. These paradoxes may be ignored or repressed, but we can neither escape from nor solve them. Such a view extends the linguistic theories of Ferdinand de Saussure, who established that the special symbol systems of natural languages are based on differences, and challenges the Western tradition of rationalist thought and its essentialist notion of certainty of meaning. For the deconstructionist, in other words, the signifier and the signified are fluid rather than fixed, and the presence of one calls forth the absence of the other. Culture, for instance, posits nature just as soul calls forth body, and neither is privileged over the other. Thus language can never be limited to meaning, and ultimate meaning is always deferred. As David H. Richter notes, "To the extent that . . . polarities [such as divine vs. human, man vs. woman, and culture vs. nature] are at the heart of Western culture, deconstruction attempts to expose the illusions upon which authority in Western culture is established" (946).

In extending the linguistic model to describe other systems, Derrida replaces concepts of thing, substance, event, and absolute with concepts of relation, ratio, construct, and relativity. According to this view, "any meaning or identity (including our own) is provisional and relative, because it is never exhaustive, it can always be traced further back to a prior network of differences, and further back again almost to infinity or the 'zero degree' of sense" (Appignanesi and Garratt 79). To convey his view that meaning includes both identity (what it is) and differences (what it is not), Derrida coined the term "différance," which includes difference, differing, deferring, deference, and deferral. Deconstruction is, then, a "strategy for revealing the underlayers of meanings 'in' a text that were suppressed or assumed in order for it to take its actual form" (Appignanesi and Garratt 80). It is an activity intended to generate skepticism about most of the doctrines we accept as truth.

Like the structuralism it challenges and even attempts to supplant, deconstruction is not solely, or even primarily, a mode of literary criticism. In fact, some deconstructionists suggest that the application of Derrida's method to literary texts in support of new interpretations is itself paradoxical because his revolutionary contribution was to apply to philosophical texts the same sort of linguistic ambiguity and fluidity characteristic of literature. Nevertheless, deconstruction has had tremendous impact on the study of literature in the postmodern era, especially since the 1970s. Prior to that time, literary criticism had been dominated by the New Criticism, which treated poetry as a complex mode of discourse, complete in and of itself, that sought to convey a truth. New Critics discovered that truth through analysis of paradox, ambiguity, and other formal elements of the work.

Deconstructionists, in contrast, posit a world of multiple, even contradictory meanings. For them, literary texts contain elements that contradict their own assertions and even their authors' intentions, and so they analyze paradox and ambiguity to disclose the way in which texts deconstruct themselves. Deconstructionists, in other words, analyze "the inconsistency between a text's grammar and its rhetoric, between its message and its activity, between what a text means and the way it goes about meaning it" (Richter 950). It is the contradictory messages of *Doctors* that make a deconstructionist reading particularly appropriate.

When Segal makes Barney the author of a book intended to reveal the truth about doctors, when he makes him, in other words, a fictive representation of himself, he calls attention to the constructed nature of his own novel. The novel may give the appearance of mirroring reality, but in truth, it is a view, indeed, it is many views, of reality or realities. The self-consciousness of Segal's narrative design here is certainly provocative, for it serves to announce his own thematic focus. Just as Barney intends in his book to humanize doctors, so, too, does Segal intend to do so in his. Yet the author's intentions, according to the deconstructionist, are frequently contradicted by the text itself, and such is the case in *Doctors*. In attempting to demythologize the myth of the doctor, Segal simultaneously calls it forth and actually enhances it. Segal's doctors— those who function as his central characters—are, in fact, superhuman.

Segal's depiction of the long and arduous process of becoming a doctor, for instance, does indeed suggest that those who practice the healing arts exemplify the highest standard of physical and mental toughness. The rigors of medical school drive at least two members of the class of 1962 to attempt suicide—one succeeds; one recovers, but only after extensive electroshock therapy. Those who survive their schooling must then run the gauntlet of an internship and residency to earn the right to practice their profession. At the midpoint of *Doctors*, Segal inserts several paragraphs of authorial commentary summarizing the process he has previously dramatized and driving home the point that doctors "have sacrificed the springtime of their lives acquiring skills to benefit their fellow man" (355). This uncharacteristic lapse into subjectivity is yet another element that draws attention to the very point that Segal is intent on challenging.

Segal's depiction of his primary doctors also contradicts his thematic intention. Laura, Barney, Bennett, and Seth are noble and idealistic. They choose the medical profession not for its financial rewards but for its ideal of service. In fact, when Barney enters private practice, he finds it difficult to sell his services and is uncomfortable having to price himself (414). Segal's doctors want the satisfaction of easing suffering and healing body and soul. They intend to be very different from the doctors of their own experience. Barney's father, as mentioned earlier, dies because a doctor fails to respond to an appeal for emergency assistance. In contrast, Barney and Bennett will both be attacked because they rush unbidden to the aid of a man choking to death.

Segal's doctors are also highly principled. They refuse to engage in the political maneuverings of their teachers and colleagues and will not be silenced by the unwritten code of the profession, the "cardinal rule that one doctor never impugns another" (515). Laura especially has no patience for ineptitude and deceit, losing two professional positions because she first criticizes the negligence and incompetence of colleagues in a Toronto hospital and later exposes the corrupt behavior of the director of the National Institutes of Health. In his own way, Seth, too, suffers for his principles. To ease the suffering of patients who will never recover, he administers the balm of death, defying religious and legal precepts to be true to his own.

In their personal lives, Segal's doctors are indeed as human as the rest of us. They feel the disappointment of unrealized dreams and the heartbreak of unhappiness in love. They know the thrill of success and the satisfaction of service. In their professional lives, however, Segal's doctors do indeed exemplify the popular notion that doctors are a breed apart, superior to the mass of humanity. Say what he likes through Barney, the novel's authorial voice, Segal includes so much evidence to the contrary that he subverts his own intention.

Although the "Acknowledgments" section of a book is not an integral part of its meaning, it is in fact a text attached to the main body of the work, and it may in fact supplement the meaning of the primary text. Such is the case in *Doctors*. In his acknowledgments, Segal names more than a dozen "good doctors" (676) who lent assistance to his project and ends with a bold affirmation of his subjects. "The medical profession," Segal asserts, "contains far more saints than sinners" (678). Here is confirmation indeed that *Doctors* simultaneously humanizes and idealizes the healer.

8

Acts of Faith
(1992)

The eternal struggle between the spiritual and the material, the secular and the sacred, is the focus of Erich Segal's sixth best-seller, *Acts of Faith* (1992). A tale of three modern pilgrims facing crises of faith, *Acts of Faith* is, according to Anthony Burgess, essentially "another love story, but it is toughened by its religious superstructure and intellectualized by its scriptural scholarship" (23). That superstructure allows Segal to explore the nature of Orthodox faith and the power of religious tradition. The love story allows him to harmonize the conflicts arising from the yearnings of the heart for both a material and a transcendent source of soul-sustaining, life-affirming belief. Both elements make *Acts of Faith* a novel that simultaneously challenges the doctrinaire but affirms the reality of true religious faith.

Acts of Faith traces the crossed destinies of three people whose lives are deeply embedded in religious communities. Daniel and Deborah Luria are the children of Rav Moses Luria, Silczer Rebbe, the hereditary spiritual leader of a small sect of Orthodox Jews living in Brooklyn. As such, their futures lie plotted before them. Daniel, of course, will eventually assume his father's position. Deborah, raised to be docile and dutiful, will be the perfect rabbi's wife. Neither, however, is willing to fulfill their father's wishes, for both have dreams of their own. Those dreams will lead them to defy their father and thereby challenge their faith through acts of independence.

When Timothy Hogan, a neighborhood tough, hurls a rock through the Lurias' front window, he shatters far more than a pane of glass. To atone for his act, he begins working as a *Shabbes goy* for the Luria household, performing on Sabbath nights the tasks that their faith prohibits them from doing themselves. An "orphan with two living parents" (7), Timothy has found solace in the Roman Catholic Church. Gradually, however, he is drawn to the quiet beauty of Deborah Luria, and she responds to his own tender strength and acute intelligence. When Rav Luria banishes Deborah to servitude in a repressive Orthodox household in Jerusalem, he believes that he has reined in his rebellious daughter, but, of course, he has not. Instead, she flees to a kibbutz, where Timothy, who is touring the Holy Land during a break in his study for the priesthood, finds her. Their acts of love will defy the barriers of their conflicting religions, but they will not surmount them. In fact, it will take pilgrimages of nearly twenty years before Deborah and Timothy, as well as Daniel, will find in love the meaning of faith and thereby resolve their personal and spiritual struggles.

PLOT DEVELOPMENT

Like Segal's other novels, *Acts of Faith* is driven almost entirely by plot, and that plot depends upon star-crossed lovers, coincidences, and deceptions—all the elements of popular fiction—for its effect. Yet as John Ottenhoff notes, "In the formulas of popular fiction can be glimpsed the timeless themes of literature" (747). Segal makes use of several. His modern pilgrims, for instance, all of whom bear allegorical names (which will be discussed in the section on character development), must progress through the materialistic maze of American culture and the hierarchical structures of religious communities, both of which challenge their faith in self and in a transcendent being. Like John Bunyan's Pilgrim in *Pilgrim's Progress*, they will be sorely tempted to sin, to sink into despair, and to renounce their faith, but their journey will instead deepen both their self-understanding and their religious sensibilities.

In the novel's father-daughter conflict, as Ottenhoff notes, Segal's plot echoes Shakespeare's *King Lear* (747). In both tales, a favored daughter who deeply loves her father refuses to submit to his will and thereby opens a breach between them. When Deborah will not promise her father to "forget this Christian" (85), he banishes her, just as Lear banished Cordelia from his life. Separated by hurt, disappointment, and equally indomitable wills, father and daughter, however, eventually reconcile, if not their differences, at least their love, and thereby testify to the power of the parental bond.

Another Shakespearean play, *Romeo and Juliet*, provides the model for Segal's own star-crossed lovers. Separated by "a bridgeless chasm between two faiths" (81), Deborah, a Jew, and Timothy, a Catholic, defy the formidable barriers of deep and profound religious differences as well as parental and communal disapproval to find their best selves in their love for one another. Unlike Romeo and Juliet, however, Segal's lovers will not be united in death only. For nearly twenty years they will live for each other only in memory and dreams as each pursues his or her own destiny, convinced that their differences cannot be overcome. The spiritual goodness of their love, however, destines them for union, and Segal's plot is thus driven by the inevitable conjunction of their lives, which has long been symbolized in their son, Eli.

One additional plot figures prominently in *Acts of Faith*—the tale of Dr. Faustus. Segal connects the classic story of a brilliant scholar who sacrifices spiritual values for material gain to Daniel's own crisis of faith. Like Faustus, the tragic hero of Christopher Marlowe's drama *Dr. Faustus* (1604), Daniel meets a charismatic figure whose promise of knowledge undermines all his previous notions about man's relationship to both the sacred and the secular. The views imparted by Professor Aaron Beller, the novel's modern Mephistopheles (or devil), give focus to the troubling questions of faith that torment Daniel. They also lead to both the spiritual dissatisfaction and the spiritual striving that characterize his life experience.

Segal's use of these classic themes and storylines may, as Ottenhoff complains, be merely "convenient, cheap ploys for the plot writer" (747). Yet from another perspective, their use relieves Segal of some of the need to delineate every aspect of character and situation. It allows him to focus instead on his primary theme of religious experience and his critique of religious doctrine (which will be discussed in the section on thematic development). As Richard M. Gardner has argued, "In some books, the words, characters, plots, etc., are trigger features which activate what we already know, or think we know, without explanation or tedious detail, but with striking emotional effect" (235). In using these classic plots for their "trigger" effects, Segal connects readers emotionally to his subject. He invites them to reexperience their own struggles between simply professing faith and actually living it and to reexamine their own questions about religious doctrine. Thus, he need not intellectualize his subject (although he does indeed provide the framework for doing so) in order to evoke and examine it.

NARRATIVE STRATEGIES: TIME, EPIGRAPHS, AND POINT OF VIEW

Time

Although Segal relies on classic plots to give shape to *Acts of Faith*, he experiments a bit with the handling of his narrative elements. Like *The Class* and *Doctors*, for instance, *Acts of Faith* ranges wide in both time and space, encompassing more than a quarter of a century and reaching from the tough streets of Brooklyn to an Israeli kibbutz, from the holy cities of Rome and Jerusalem to the slums of Brasília. In those other novels, Segal grounded his narrative in historical time, using references to world events and actual persons to situate his plots and characters and thereby control the reader's sense of time's passage.

Acts of Faith, however, lacks that specificity. An occasional mention of a specific year or a brief allusion, or reference, to an historical event such as the Six-Day War of 1967 suggests that Daniel, Deborah, and Timothy live their childhood and adolescence in 1950s Brooklyn, but were it not for references to electric lights and other modern conveniences such as air-conditioning, it could just as easily be the 1920s or even the 1890s. The focus on the Lurias' strict, Orthodox lifestyle, especially their habits of dress and what Segal characterizes as their repressive treatment of women, which includes arranged marriages of teenage daughters, gives the novel an otherworldly, ahistorical quality. This vagueness about real time emphasizes the universality of the characters' struggles. More important, it provides a subtle commentary on these Orthodox customs, suggesting their anachronistic nature. Within the world of the novel, such outdated customs seem to have less to do with faith and more to do with control of the faithful.

Epigraphs

Like *The Class* and *Doctors*, *Acts of Faith* is also divided into a number of sections, each of which delimits a stage of development in the characters' lives. In *Acts of Faith*, however, Segal foregoes the customary epigraphs with which he usually announces the major theme of his novels' various sections. Instead, he uses only one epigraph, or quotation, at the beginning of the entire novel, a passage from St. Augustine's *Confessions*, the singularity of which emphasizes its connection to the novel's major theme: "Too late came I to love you, O Beauty both so ancient and so new! Too late came I to love you—and behold you were within me all the time. . . ." Its elegiac tone of regret for what is lost or perceived as lost anticipates the resolution of Deborah and Timothy's forbidden relationship (the significance of which is explained in the section on thematic development) in the spirituality of love, a divine force that elevates even its human expression into an act of faith.

Point of View

Segal's most innovative change in narrative strategy involves the novel's structure and point of view. Each section of *Acts of Faith* is comprised of a series of randomly alternating chapters devoted in almost equal number to each of the three major characters. Segal privileges Daniel's voice in this arrangement by making him a first person, or "I," narrator. For Deborah's and Timothy's sections, Segal uses the third person, or omniscient, narrator.

At its best, the random arrangement of the chapters disrupts the sequence of events and thereby delays the revelation of key plot elements and controls the pace of the narrative. At its worst, the haphazard chapter arrangement is merely a ploy to eliminate transitions. The narrative strategy relieves Segal of the necessity to connect one episode to the next. Moreover, the tactic is more frustrating than effective. Just as readers become engaged by Deborah's struggle to assert her independence or moved by Timothy's sad farewell to his mother, the scene abruptly shifts to another character, a different event, severing their attachment to the narrative.

Segal's use of dual points of view is similarly ineffective. Use of the first person narrator gives Daniel's episodes a certain poignancy, conveying the painful confusion of a man who has lost his faith but needs desperately to believe by making the reader privy to his innermost thoughts and feelings. It does not, however, make Daniel the novel's central figure, as a first-person narrative tends to do. In fact, Segal may have used the first-person narrator here in an unsuccessful attempt to prevent Deborah's and Timothy's stories from overwhelming Daniel's.

Segal's decision to tell Deborah's and Timothy's stories in the third person gives their struggles less immediacy and intimacy. Perhaps the object was to temper the emotionalism of their love story (which it does not, given its predominance in the plot) by enhancing the intellectual basis of their crises of faith. If so, the strategy fails because it denies readers the opportunity to share Deborah's and Timothy's reflections about their faith. Timothy's decision to publish the book by the controversial priest Ernesto Hardt, for instance, would certainly make more sense if readers could enter into his deliberations about an act that will surely jeopardize his position in the Church. The novel's dual points of view ultimately serve no real purpose. The shifting narrative perspectives are as random as the shifting chapters.

CHARACTER DEVELOPMENT

The protagonists, or central characters, of *Acts of Faith* are modern pilgrims facing crises of faith both secular and sacred. Although Daniel, Deborah, and Timothy never truly doubt the reality and power of God, they do mistrust their own ability to live the tenets of their respective faiths because they are unwilling to accept without question the very tenets that they are expected to live. Each thus finds both comfort and pain in the religious faith that sustains his or her being, and Segal's characterizations focus on the tensions created by these contradictory responses. As the characters struggle to resolve them, they find the will to believe not only in God but also in themselves, no matter the rituals of their worship.

Segal uses the novel's prologue, three short chapters focusing on each of his central characters, to establish the defining personality trait of each. Fear, for instance, lies at the core of Daniel's being, the self-paralyzing fear of failure that arises from the desire to please others. As the answer to his father's fervent prayers, Daniel understands almost from the beginning of awareness his privileged position as the only son among Rav Moses Luria's four children. More important, he "could sense," even before he entered school, "the burden of my father's expectations" (6). "Born a prince" (5), Daniel knows that he is destined to be the next Silczer Rebbe, the spiritual leader of a small sect of Orthodox Jews, and thus his life and his behavior are circumscribed by the force of another. When the Irish-Catholic boys in the neighborhood assault him on his way to school, for instance, Daniel stands passive, protecting but not defending himself from their verbal and physical abuse. The son of Rav Moses Luria, after all, must not disgrace his family or his faith. Throughout his son's childhood and even into his adulthood, Rav Moses will "cast a long shadow over [Daniel's] life" (18), and Daniel will find it difficult to shape his own image.

Although Daniel and his father share a deep love of learning, education will, rather ironically, drive a wedge between them. In his youth, Daniel had occasionally chafed under some of his father's restrictions and even disagreed with some of his decisions and actions, especially his efforts to arrange a marriage for Deborah and his eventual banishment of her, but he had never challenged his rule. He begins his rabbinical studies determined to fulfill his father's expectations, although he shares with his classmates, many of whom are also the sons of rabbis, the "fear that we will never be the men our fathers are" (119). But contact with conflicting ideological perspectives, especially those of Professor Aaron Beller, inevitably exacerbates Daniel's self-doubts.

Descended from a line of distinguished rabbis, Beller is a modern Mephistopheles, or devil, whose "revolutionary, rebellious notions" (127) about faith Daniel deliberately confronts when he enrolls in his Psychology of Religion course. Like his counterpart in *Dr. Faustus*, Beller promises Daniel knowledge. In accepting the gift, however, Daniel compromises his faith. When Beller participates in an exorcism performed on Daniel's half sister Rena, not because he believes that evil has possessed her but because she believes that it has, Daniel begins to see faith through the eyes of his teacher. For Daniel, the "pagan ceremony" (166) confirms Beller's view that "blind faith" is "irrational, neurotic, or a sublimation of erotic impulse" (131). He sees his father "grow helpless in the grip of atavistic superstition" (166) and realizes that he cannot follow him into that world (167).

Daniel's crisis of faith (254) drives him to abandon his rabbinical studies and thereby fail his father. In fact, when Daniel announces his decision, Rav Moses disowns him—and then suffers a stroke from which he never entirely recovers. Estranged from a personal touchstone of belief and bereft of the spirituality of faith, Daniel transforms himself into Dan Lurie and pursues material gain as a substitute for all that he has lost. Such a compromise, however, fails to satisfy Daniel's longings for meaning and purpose beyond the self, and he spends much of his adult life struggling to reconcile his doubts. Eventually, of course, he embraces the role for which he was indeed destined, but not until he recovers his faith in himself.

If Daniel's defining character trait is fear, his sister Deborah's is anger. Her memories of early childhood, as the novel's prologue makes clear, are dominated by acts of exclusion. Whereas the family celebrated Daniel's birth with the ritual of circumcision, there had been no celebration to mark her birth, although her mother assured her that the absence "doesn't mean we don't love you just as much" (12). Whereas Daniel studied the Talmud, Deborah was schooled by a "specially abridged version [of the Code of Laws] compiled for women in the nineteenth century" that was intended to make her a perfect Jewish wife (13). Whereas Daniel and the other men and boys, in keeping with Orthodox tradition, were called to read the Torah (the first five books of the Old Testament) in synagogue, Deborah and the other women and girls were relegated to worship behind a curtain on the balcony and not permitted to read the Torah. Such acts of exclusion make Deborah resentful and impatient, especially because they signify the most cutting exclusion of all. Deeply religious, she is hurt and angry that she will never be permitted to "serve God to the fullest because she had not been born a man" (14).

Although her sense of self has been developed within a rigid culture that confines a woman's role to maintaining a Jewish home, Deborah refuses to accept this limitation, and thus her life is shaped by acts of rebellion. Attracted by the keen intelligence and gentle, respectful habits of Timothy, the *Shabbes goy* who enters the family home each Friday evening, she engages in forbidden conversation with him. Later exiled to Jerusalem for her subsequent sins, she causes a riot at the Wailing Wall because she sings her faith too loudly and incites the other women to join her (123–25). Escaping from her captivity, she joins a kibbutz, where she is valued for herself, encouraged to develop her talents, and introduced to a liberal understanding of her faith. Eventually, Deborah defies convention and parental disapproval and musters the courage to pursue her true desire. She becomes the rabbi in the Luria family. Deborah's acts of rebellion thus reveal the depth of her anger and resentment, the strength of her will. Their source is a profound wish to be included within the circle of her faith rather than exiled to its periphery.

Deborah's will and faith are sorely tested by her love for two men—her father and Timothy Hogan. Like Daniel, Deborah has no real desire to hurt Rav Moses, nor does she wish to disobey or shame him. In fact, although "she believed she had severed all emotional ties, the little girl in her still wanted Papa's approval" (234), in spite of everything that had come between them. When her father suffers his stroke, Deborah, a prodigal daughter, returns to the family fold, bringing with her her young son, Eli. Yet the essential conflict between father and daughter persists. She cannot, for instance, reveal to him the true subject of her studies, for she knows that he would never approve of her rabbinical ordination. Moreover, because she fears his influence on the grandson to whom he has transferred his dynastic dreams, she and Eli move into an apartment provided by Daniel, who understands her fears for Eli and supports her goal. Deborah's need for her father's approval tempts her to become the dutiful daughter, to subordinate her being to him and his beliefs, but she ultimately determines to thrive on self-affirmation. Anything else forces her to be dishonest.

Deborah's love for Timothy Hogan is as strong as her will to believe, which is exactly why it poses such problems for her. Deborah responds to the same qualities in Timothy that she herself possesses—intelligence, reverence for faith, sensitivity, strength. When she and Timothy express their spiritual union in the physical act of love, both are convinced of its absolute rightness. Yet they are equally certain that they cannot live their love together. In fact, neither asks the other for a commitment because each understands what the other would have to surrender to make such a commitment. Neither will ask the other to deny his or her sustaining religious faith, for to do so would be to sacrifice the heart's core.

Like Deborah, Timothy, too, is fueled by anger and possesses a "fighting spirit" (8). Its source, as the prologue makes clear, is his unhappy home life. Although both of his parents are living, he has never known either of them and learns as a child that he is, in fact, the bastard son of an unnamed father. Raised by his aunt and uncle, he had received from them nothing but hostility and resentment, both of which he had learned to reciprocate. More than anything else in life, Timothy had wanted to be loved, yet he despaired of ever finding someone to love him. And then one night he seeks sanctuary from his loneliness and pain in the parish church, and there, in answer to his prayer, the Virgin comforts him with a profession of love. The experience shapes Timothy's future.

Within the Church, Timothy learns to contain his anger, to repress the violent outbursts that had once led him to hurl a rock through the window of Rav Moses Luria's home. He rises quickly in the Roman Catholic hierarchy, studying in Rome, working in the Vatican, and eventually undertaking a sensitive mission to Brazil to investigate a renegade priest. Clearly being groomed for the papacy, Timothy appears to have found the peace of love. Yet he cannot forget that he had once known the passion of love as well. He cannot forget that he and Deborah Luria had shared a sacred love, and that knowledge haunts his very being. Timothy will ultimately have to acknowledge that his devotion to the Church is driven by "frantic desperation. He wanted to escape, renounce the world, and thereby exorcize all thoughts of Deborah Luria" (99). He will ultimately have to choose between his faith and the Church.

To enrich his characterizations, Segal gives Daniel, Deborah, and Timothy allusive and appropriate biblical names. Daniel, for instance, was one of three Jewish captives chosen to serve the Babylonian king during the Hebrew exile. Strong in his faith, the biblical Daniel insists on being loyal to Jewish traditions, refusing to eat meat that is not kosher and to bow to the king's statue.

The biblical Daniel's steadfastness to Jewish tradition provides the context for what may be the most curious aspect of the novel—Daniel Luria's return to his Orthodox faith. The motivation for his action is virtually unexplored or at best attributed rather unsatisfactorily to his instantaneous love for the Orthodox Miriam, the woman he eventually marries. By connecting Daniel to his biblical namesake, however, Segal indicates from the novel's beginning that the son of Rav Moses Luria will indeed remain true to his faith and to its tradition of worship. Daniel will inhabit the lion's den. He will live in his lover Ariel's lavish apartment, thrive on her masterpiece paintings and insider stock tips, and nearly lose his soul to the emptiness of the material world. But just as faith protects the biblical Daniel, so, too, does it ultimately save his namesake.

The biblical names of Deborah and Timothy are equally appropriate, underscoring aspects of their characters and foreshadowing events in their lives. When Timothy pays homage to a teenage Deborah by reciting "The Song of Deborah" from the Book of Judges, he invites comparisons between the women. The biblical Deborah was the only female judge in a patriarchal, or male-dominated, society. Endowed with prophetic voice, she is strong-willed and capable of leading Hebrew troops into victory against the Philistines (137). Like her namesake, Deborah Luria will defy the Hebrew patriarchal tradition and become a rabbi, a leader of the faithful. Moreover, the passage that Timothy recites, "Awake, awake, Deborah; Awake, awake, utter a song" (81), foreshadows the riot at the Wailing Wall precipitated by Deborah's singing.

Similarly, Timothy Hogan is linked to his biblical namesake by act and vocation. Converted to Christianity by the Apostle Paul, the biblical Timothy became one of Paul's missionary associates and, despite his youth, earned a position of authority in the church and helped to formulate its structure. Timothy's equally youthful contemporary namesake will rise within that structure as well as undertake missions for the Church hierarchy. Their efforts on behalf of the church thus define their lives.

Among the novel's minor characters, only Rav Moses Luria plays a major role in the lives of Daniel, Deborah, and Timothy. Certainly, Professor Aaron Beller leads Daniel into a profound sense of doubt, and late in the novel, Ernesto Hardt, a renegade priest, similarly challenges Timothy by introducing him to liberation theology, or the belief that the Church should engage in revolutionary social action. Deborah also discovers a place for herself within her religion under the guidance of the kibbutz leader Boaz and Rabbis Steve and Esther Goldman. All of these minor characters embody alternate faiths; they affront religious traditions and yet remain true to their faiths. They are significant, however, only because the powerful force of Rav Moses stands in opposition to them.

As the spiritual leader of his congregation, Rav Moses is a figure of religious authority and thus functions symbolically in the novel. As a rabbi, he interprets God's Word and Jewish law and leads the congregants in worship, accorded his power and position by virtue of his wisdom and learning. As rabbi to his children, he is inextricably entwined with their understanding of Judaism, eventually coming to embody for them its precepts and creeds. Because Rav Moses assumes this role in the novel, the discord between father and children within the Luria family signifies the spiritual struggles of Daniel and Deborah. Like an Old Testament God, Rav Moses commands his children to obey Jewish law, but they cannot obey without question. (Nor, for that matter, will Timothy, following his mission to Brazil, accept without challenge the precepts of his Church.) Their individual will to believe cannot overcome their need to understand, so each of them struggles with his or her earthly father and, by extension, his or her Heavenly Father. They equate the blessing of one as assurance of the blessing of the other, but eventually they learn to separate them and to honor both by remaining true to themselves. They must be faithful in their own ways.

THEMATIC DEVELOPMENT

The spiritual struggles of Segal's central characters serve as the basis for a critical examination of organized religion that is the thematic focus of *Acts of Faith*. To develop his theme, Segal, according to Ottenhoff, "pursues some troubling issues: How can any church continue to exclude women from full and equal participation? How can any religious community continue to deny the power of sexuality and maintain rules of celibacy?" (747). How, in other words, can the faithful live their faith as human beings in the material world? Segal's answers to these questions have not always pleased church authorities. In fact, several Roman Catholic newspapers rejected ads for the book because it challenged the doctrine of celibacy and championed liberation theology ("Ads" 12). They are, however, answers that do indeed affirm the place of faith within the physical and spiritual lives of men and women.

Segal's depiction of Orthodox Jewish life is certainly problematic. On the one hand, it sustains a community of faith capable of surviving the material values and spiritual malaise so prevalent in the modern world. In their celebration of the Sabbath and their participation in ancient rites and rituals, the Lurias draw strength from religious tradition and avoid the traps of modern life—the materialism and the skepticism—that have ensnared, respectively, Ariel and Professor Beller, preventing them from finding peace and happiness. On the other hand, the rites and rituals practiced by these Orthodox Jews conceal intellectual dishonesty and harbor superstition. When Daniel begins his rabbinical studies, for instance, he must acknowledge that his father's spiritual leadership is based on a selective reading of the Torah, one that upheld its Orthodox practices and ignored contradictory evidence or views. Despite scholarly tradition, some sects of ultra-Orthodox Judaism also sanction exorcisms and condone belief in *dybbuks*, or demons. Orthodox tradition, as Segal depicts it, also devalues and marginalizes women.

To a modern woman like Deborah, this tradition causes frustration and unhappiness. Sensitive and intelligent, Deborah wants nothing more than to live her faith and serve her God, but as an Orthodox woman, her choices are limited. Orthodox women perform their most valuable function by maintaining Jewish homes, but such a role is too confining for Deborah. Moreover, the marital customs and sexual prohibitions that other Orthodox women accept make Deborah feel inferior, and she chafes under the restrictions that deny her full expression of her faith in worship. Segal is clearly sympathetic to Deborah's feelings, depicting her situation as unjust and even debilitating. In so doing, he suggests that Orthodox tradition may not only harm Jewish women but also deny others the benefit of their talents.

Segal's examination of Roman Catholicism challenges some of its most deeply held traditions as well, especially its insistence on celibacy. Timothy's love of Deborah does not prevent him from serving God, as his rise in the Church hierarchy clearly indicates. It does not compromise his intelligence or his sensitivity, nor does it undermine his faith. Timothy, Segal suggests, may even be a better priest because he loves Deborah. Love is the "human tie" (524) through which men and women know God. It expresses faith rather than diminishes it, a lesson that Timothy learns from Ernesto Hardt, a priest whose compassion for the poor and suffering in Brasília is matched by his love for his wife and children. Hardt's flaunting of Church policy simply does not prevent him from ministering in the name of God.

Ernesto Hardt's example also underscores for Timothy the emptiness of Vatican politics. In Rome, among the Church hierarchy, Timothy is far removed from direct ministry to the faithful. In fact, he finds himself courting the city's aristocracy and enforcing Vatican policies as he is thrust into a subtle competition for the papacy. In Brasília's slums, and under Hardt's guidance, however, Timothy touches the lives of people who need the comfort of the Church both spiritually and materially. There he finds a mission that matters. Under Hardt's influence, Timothy begins to question Vatican politics and policies, but he returns to Rome believing that he can enlist his advocates in Hardt's social ministry. When he finds that they are far more interested in church politics than in church mission, he realizes that far more than physical distance separates Rome and Brasília. The discovery leads Timothy to reconsider not his faith, but his vocation.

Acts of Faith's depiction of orthodox religious communities, Jewish and Roman Catholic, is neither flattering nor comforting. As Segal sees them, they are both authoritarian and hierarchical, offering little opportunity for individual expressions of faith. In fact, they seem designed to compel their congregants' obedience to church dicta rather than to nurture their spirituality. To Segal, these communities marginalize and even demean a large portion of the faithful on the basis of their sex, sanctioning traditions such as celibacy and patriarchal privilege that deny both men and women the opportunity to achieve their full humanity.

It is within this context that Segal's depiction of alternate religious communities resonates so persuasively. On the kibbutz and within the Reform congregation that Deborah joins in New York, the congregants live their faith amid the joy of fellowship and for the benefit of the community. Laughter and song accompany even the most menial tasks, for they are performed as acts of love and acts of faith. Amid the squalor of Brasília's slums, the spirit of the religious life persists as well in the commitment to social justice and the missionary zeal of the faithful. In these communities, love can flourish and bind one to another; in these communities, every person can express the better part of his or her common humanity. In these communities, the needs of the body and the soul are simultaneously fulfilled. In his positive depiction of these alternate religious communities, Segal clearly advocates for a living faith, an inclusive faith, a faith that affirms the humanity of every person and nurtures the gifts and talents of all.

A CULTURAL CRITIQUE OF *ACTS OF FAITH*

For the cultural critic, *Acts of Faith* offers some provocative insights into concepts of ethnicity and American identity. The cultural critic, whose theoretical positions are more fully explained in chapter 5, views literature as an expression of culture and the novel as a sociological document. Thus, Segal's focus on Orthodox Judaism and Roman Catholicism has much to say about their status in American society. Those who practice these faiths have clearly not been assimilated into the mainstream Protestantism that has long been considered a defining force in American society. In a nation that advocates a melting-pot ideology, however, minority religions are under tremendous social pressure to abandon or minimize truly divisive differences of belief and practice and to emphasize instead common traditions of faith. A melting-pot ideology, in other words, tends to democratize religious faith, to transform all denominations into American denominations. *Acts of Faith* gives evidence of this transformation.

As hyphenated Americans, Daniel, Deborah, and Timothy straddle two cultures. Within their Jewish- and Irish-American communities, they speak the language, enact the rituals, and share the values of their groups. Indeed, their communities exist to preserve their ethnic heritage, of which religion is a primary component. Beyond their communities, these hyphenated Americans meet mistrust of their rituals and resistance to their ways, not only from the dominant group but also from other ethnic groups. Daniel, for instance, dreads his ventures into "enemy territory," the Irish-American neighborhood where he is victimized by Timothy and the other local toughs. The more foreign their culture, the more likely they are to meet such resistance.

Because it cuts so close to the heart's core, to the essence of a person's identity, religion is one of the most contested grounds of ethnicity, especially if the believer feels pressure to adapt to dominant beliefs and practices different than his or her own. Religion defines the individual's values and attitudes. It shapes his or her worldview. It even determines the nature of personal relationships such as marriage and parenthood. Religious differences thus have the potential to drive a wedge between people who might otherwise share common interests and goals. Religious differences may, in fact, inhibit the ethnic's assimilation into the dominant culture and the development of a national identity, the traditional goal of the American melting-pot ideology.

As members of an Orthodox religious community, Daniel and Deborah are more Jewish than American. Their lives are circumscribed by Jewish customs and religious rituals. Their clothing and hairstyles, the visible signs of their ethnicity, ensure their exclusion from the dominant community by announcing their rejection of it. Yet because they are Americans, they have absorbed enough of the national identity to make their Jewishness sit uneasily on their shoulders. Deborah especially chafes under religious prohibitions and wants the freedom to choose her own mate, the freedom to develop her individual identity. Her escape to the kibbutz is the perfect declaration of independence for this hyphenated American, for it permits her to acknowledge both her ethnic and her national identity. She has the freedom to be herself within her faith.

Timothy's decision to enter the priesthood functions similarly. It separates him from the dominant community, subordinating national identity to religious affiliation. Such affiliation, however, requires that Timothy repress something of his essential self and suppress his individual needs, especially his need to love and to be loved for himself. It requires, in other words, that Timothy define himself solely as a Roman Catholic.

For the ethnic American, religion may be a barrier to assimilation, for its tenets sometimes stand in opposition to national values such as liberty, equality, and individuality. It need not, however, be an insurmountable barrier. As a living thing, it need only to adapt its message, to emphasize the shared values of church and nation. It need only to be democratized, and here, Deborah's Reform congregation and Hardt's renegade community serve as models. Enlightened and modern, they practice equality and encourage self-actualization. Their commitment to social justice also expands their sense of community, fostering an inclusiveness that dissolves boundaries. In America, Protestantism, Roman

Catholicism, Judaism, all the world's faiths are transformed in the melting pot into distinctly American versions that even make interfaith marriage acceptable.

It is within this context that Timothy and Deborah's love resonates most fully. In fact, it is the very symbol of the melting-pot ideology. By transcending religious affiliation, but living their faiths, Deborah and Timothy affirm nonsectarian, humane values that make possible a new order of the faithful. The birth of their son, Eli, the product of the melting pot, promises to perpetuate this hybridity. *Acts of Faith* thus testifies to the nature of religion in America. Orthodoxy, as Daniel's example suggests, will not disappear, but democratization and hybridity are both desirable and inevitable.

In the end, *Acts of Faith* affirms love as the source of true religious feeling. Through love we embrace the world and those who inhabit it; through love we experience the spiritual; through love we know God. From love come the acts of faith that give meaning to our existence. Segal may not, as Ottenhoff observes, bring to his examination the intellectual rigor of serious authors such as Isaac Bashevis Singer, Bernard Malamud, or Mary Gordon, all of whom have written sensitive and complex novels about the life of faith for the Jew or the Catholic (747). By attaching such an examination to popular plots, however, he does indeed engage a vast audience in the debate.

9

Prizes
(1995)

"Behind every Nobel Prize there is not merely a lab book, but a saga. Of personal sacrifice, of pain, of disappointment, and rarely—very rarely—of unadulterated joy" (447). So begins the final chapter of Erich Segal's seventh best-seller, *Prizes* (1995), a "saga" of three scientific careers. To demonstrate the truth of his observation, Segal explores the lives and probes the minds of a physicist, an immunologist, and a geneticist to reveal both the personal and the professional costs and rewards of dedication to scientific discovery. As his saga demonstrates, the mysteries of the universe and the enigmas of life itself may compel the scientific genius to seek answers, but the human need to achieve greatness and the desire for recognition are equally powerful forces in the quest for knowledge. Science is not, in other words, a purely objective, coldly clinical pursuit, but rather a process deeply human and thus as stimulating and frustrating as existence.

Prizes is the story of three parallel lives. Adam Coopersmith, a brilliant physician and immunologist who genuinely cares about his patients, devotes his career to eliminating the scourge of childlessness. In the laboratory, he works tirelessly to produce a drug that will suppress an antivirus that prevents many women from becoming pregnant, driven by the satisfaction he takes in giving life to their hopes and dreams. For all his success, however, he must face one bitter failure: His therapy cannot help the woman he loves. In yet another laboratory, Sandy Raven, a geneticist, labors to reverse the aging process in cells. Once before, early in his career, Sandy should have shared a Nobel Prize, but he had been betrayed by his own trust in others. The bitter lesson cost Sandy his wife and child as well as his faith in people and his joy in life. Isabel da Costa is a child prodigy who grows up to be a brilliant theoretical physicist. A toddler who teaches herself to read, Isabel begins her undergraduate studies at Berkeley at the age of twelve, driven by her own acute intelligence and the relentless prodding of her father, Ray. By the age of twenty-three, she has disproved the existence of the Fifth Force and develops a formula for the Unified Field Theory that baffled Albert Einstein for the last twenty years of his life. Isabel's professional achievements, however, come at the cost of a childhood. One of her most difficult challenges, therefore, will be to exert all her force of character and intelligence to assert her independence and to reclaim her own life. Although the lives of Segal's three scientists take singular paths, their destinies converge in Sweden, where the promise of the Nobel Prize casts its seductive power. Their individual journeys to that ultimate reward drive the plot of *Prizes*.

NARRATIVE STRATEGIES: PLOT AND POINT OF VIEW

Plot

Like Segal's other novels, *Prizes* is developed primarily in cinematic style. The novel consists of a series of sixty-three randomly organized chapters, each focusing on one of the major characters, a prologue, and an epilogue. Together, the chapters form three parallel narratives. The stories of Isabel and Adam account for the majority of the chapters. Sandy's story unfolds in fifteen chapters, and Anya, Adam's wife, is the focus of one chapter. Were the novel a film, each chapter would function as a scene, for each is a discrete and unified whole. Moreover, the juxtaposition of chapters creates the sense of continuity between the episodes. The expository connections, whether explanatory transitions or authorial commentary, are virtually nonexistent. The technique gives the novel, as Eric Korn notes, an "undeniable narrative thrust" (29).

One effect of the parallel narrative structure is to obscure the novel's sense of real time. The stories of each character begin at different points in his or her individual life and seem to run concurrently. By the novel's conclusion, Isabel is approximately twenty-three years old, Sandy is about forty, and Adam is nearing fifty. Isabel's extreme youth and obvious maturing process, however, tend to add years to Sandy and Adam, making them seem older than they are intended to be. So, too, does the fact that they begin life in the novel as adults. Were these parallel stories dramatized in a film, their synchronicity would certainly be clear, yet because "the characters," as Korn notes, "seem to age differentially, the chronology of events makes uneasy reading" (29).

Cinematic style is only one of the strategies Segal uses to control his narrative. He also propels it by adding an element of mystery to the plot. The novel's title leads readers to expect that a competition for the Nobel Prize will figure prominently in the lives of the major characters, and throughout the novel, the single unanswered question is "Who will win?" Segal maintains suspense about the answer by making clear that the achievement of each of his scientists is deserving of such recognition. He also teases readers early in the novel when the prize is virtually snatched from the hands of Sandy Raven by his unscrupulous mentor. By the end of the novel, Segal adds one other twist to the quest for the prize—politics. In dramatizing its nominating and voting process, Segal makes it clear that the Nobel Prize is frequently awarded to the individual who mounts the best campaign or who has the most powerful connections. Doubts and complications thus keep readers in suspense about the winners' identities until the novel's final pages.

Point of View

Segal elects to use a limited omniscient narrator, an all-knowing voice capable of entering the characters' thoughts, describing their feelings, and relating past experiences with as much authority as present circumstances. Consequently, it is nearly impossible to differentiate one character from another through dialogue. Their individual voices lack singularity of personality. Yet Segal occasionally makes an effort to provide an alternative voice or perspective.

Twice Segal inserts journalistic stories to convey information about his characters. He introduces readers to Sandy, for instance, by reproducing the *Time* magazine "cover story" that trumpets his discovery of a treatment to reverse the aging process. While the information in the article is, of course, important in and of itself, of greater import is the fact that Sandy merits a cover story. Segal trusts that his readers recognize that the magazine's cover usually features world leaders, captains of business and industry, or significant events, so the selection of a self-proclaimed "nerd" (18) highlights the importance of the reluctant celebrity. Similarly, Segal inserts a newspaper story about Isabel's first day of classes at Berkeley. The wire service report underscores both the phenomenal nature of Isabel's achievement and the shadow of sensationalism dogging her existence. Both stories also contribute to the novel's sense of realism and tone of objectivity, reinforcing, in other words, the omniscient voice.

Throughout the narrative, Segal also includes passages from Isabel's diary to reveal her most private thoughts and feelings. Because Raymond da Costa fiercely guards his child genius, Isabel rarely speaks in her own voice. For much of her life, she subordinates her needs and desires in an effort to please her beloved father, so she speaks his desires time after time. Isabel's diary, however, reveals the private self, especially the pain of separation from loved ones, the frightening passage into womanhood, the isolation of genius. The journal entries that Segal writes for Isabel generally lack the ring of authenticity because they are seldom different in rhythm and vocabulary from the authorial voice. Yet they do provide insight into the prodigy's inner life and prepare the reader for her eventual emancipation.

CHARACTER DEVELOPMENT

Prizes is essentially a plot-driven novel. Although its action unfolds over a period of approximately twenty years, the essential natures of its characters change little during that time. Nevertheless, their individual triumphs and tragedies are compelling, and Segal invests their lives with a touching humanity, allowing readers to see both their strengths and their weaknesses. Most true of all in *Prizes*, however, is the fact that scientific genius is no guarantee of personal happiness.

A man whose brilliance is matched by his compassion, Adam Coopersmith is indeed a rare human being. Generous with both his time and his talent, Adam runs his laboratory at the Massachusetts Institute of Technology (MIT) as a collaborative venture. At daily brown-bag lunches, he encourages his colleagues to share their insights and their conundrums, nurturing communal purpose and goals. Ego figures hardly at all in Adam's quest for answers. A physician, he is motivated instead by humanitarian impulses, by a desire to eliminate the diseases and ailments that impinge on the quality of human life (20–21).

Family life is important to Adam (88), perhaps because his own child-hood had been the source of so much unhappiness. When his mother died in childbirth, twelve-year-old Adam had virtually raised himself, for his steelworker father showed nothing but disdain for the son who rejected his values and blamed him for his mother's death (30). Adam survived his childhood by learning to dive. For one brief perfect moment, as he soared into space from the platform, he could be utterly alone with himself, utterly in control of his life. Such mastery of self characterizes Adam Coopersmith.

When he marries, Adam seeks to build the perfect family life and to model his marriage on that of his substitute parents, Max and Lisl Rudolph. His wife, Toni, however, is a former Washington lawyer more interested in the dynamics of political power than the joys of domesticity. Following the birth of their daughter Heather, Toni devotes herself to her career, Adam devotes himself to Heather, and the couple grow apart. Divorce is inevitable, especially when Adam finds himself drawn to the warm gentleness and sensitive intelligence of a Russian émigré, Anya Avilova. It will, however, cost him greatly, as Toni exacts her revenge by winning sole custody of their daughter. Adam and Anya will forge a strong marriage, but a childless one, for he, rather ironically, can do nothing to correct her inability to conceive. Thus, the man to whom family means all, for whom children give meaning to his science, must bear his own personal failure.

Like Adam, Sandy Raven also has his share of personal unhappiness, but he tends to retreat into the sanctuary of his laboratory rather than risk the inevitable failures and hurts of life. A lonely and insecure boy who develops into a solitary and mistrustful man, Sandy has found personal affirmation from only two sources—the lab and his father. His scientific discoveries confirm his intelligence and provide some purpose to his life. His father, a Hollywood producer of B movies, provides emotional support and encouragement. In fact, from the time his wife deserted the family, Sidney Raven has been the one constant in his son's life, and Sandy will do anything to protect him.

Naive and idealistic, Sandy invests his hopes and dreams in others, thereby creating the conditions for his own betrayal. Sandy's mentor at MIT, for instance, Gregory Morgenstern, quickly becomes the young scientist's intellectual and spiritual father. Side by side in the laboratory, the two develop mutual respect and affection, and their relationship is thoroughly cemented when Sandy "[falls] in love not merely with the Morgensterns' daughter but with their values" (236).

The Morgenstern values, however, are not, as Sandy learns, incorruptible. When Morgenstern takes credit for his assistant's discovery (288), Sandy loses not only his rightful share in a Nobel Prize but also his wife and daughter, for Judy supports her father rather than her husband in the affair. Disillusioned and disheartened, Sandy flees MIT for the West Coast and buries himself in work, becoming secretive and mistrustful and determined that all his future "research would be motivated by advancement and rewarded with material gain" (307).

The other repository of Sandy's hopes and dreams is Kim Tower, a Hollywood starlet turned studio executive whom he had worshipped since high school. As Rochelle Taubman, she had captivated her gawky classmate, so much so that "he did not feel the slightest bit exploited" when she "cajoled" him into tutoring her for their math and science exams (51). Later, Sandy intercedes with his father to help Rochelle get her break in Hollywood. Following her metamorphosis into Kim Tower, Sandy follows with keen interest the rise and fall and rise of her career. To him, she is a goddess who embodies all his dreams. To possess her is to achieve the only real success that matters.

Yet Rochelle, who is as superficial as a Hollywood set, is no goddess. In fact, she is hard and manipulative, incapable of any kindness or generosity of spirit. When she ruthlessly fires his father, Sandy can no longer allow himself to be deceived. She is no different from Morgenstern in her callous disregard of others. This time, however, Sandy does not retreat from betrayal, but rather fights it. His victory is an act of self-assertion as momentous as any of his scientific discoveries.

Unlike Sandy, who retreats from hurt and betrayal, Isabel da Costa, the child prodigy who develops into a famous theoretical physicist by the age of twenty-three, is utterly fearless. No theory is sacred to her; no enigma is too challenging. Her fierce intelligence compels her to seek answers to the mysteries of the universe, and her strong sense of self gives her the courage to take her place in the scientific community when age alone should deny her access. The twelve-year-old girl who so deftly handles the press on her first day at Berkeley is equally adept at delivering, in Italian, her acceptance speech when she receives, at age eighteen, the Enrico Fermi Prize in physics. Intellectually, Isabel knows no bounds. Emotionally, however, she is every bit her age.

The source of Isabel's most profound disappointment is her complicated relationship with her father. From the moment he recognizes his daughter's remarkable intellect, Raymond da Costa assumes control of her life, accelerating the pace of her learning and "cocooning her from intrusions and distractions" (292) that might interfere with the achievement of her potential. Eager to please the father who has sacrificed his life to hers, Isabel submits to his rule, even at the cost of her own happiness. When her mother, for instance, encourages Isabel to develop her natural musical talent, Raymond disapproves, so mother and daughter must steal moments of mutual pleasure playing the violin when he is away from home and then feel guilty when he inevitably discovers their frivolity. Similarly, when Isabel begins her undergraduate studies, Raymond makes it clear to his wife that she and their son Peter will not accompany father and daughter to Berkeley, thereby ending for all intents and purposes any semblance of real family life for his daughter. As much as Isabel might yearn for her mother's comfort and guidance and her brother's companionship, she cannot deny her father's wishes. Consequently, Isabel's accomplishments are always accompanied by a vague sense of disappointment, by a wistful longing for something more in her life.

In the course of the novel, Isabel feels the wrath of the scientific community when she dismantles the theoretical underpinnings for the existence of the Fifth Force, and she learns a shocking secret that nearly shatters her existence. Yet nothing is more difficult or traumatic for Isabel than her assertion of independence from her father. When, during her trip to Italy to accept the Fermi Prize, Isabel slips away from the awards ceremony—and her father—to purchase with her prize money a hand-crafted antique violin for her mother, she tips the balance of power in her personal life. Until this point, she has concealed from her father the depth of her feelings for her advisor's son, Jerry Pracht, and she has never committed one rebellious act. In failing to consult him about her decision, however, in arranging all the details of the purchase, in pleasing herself by pleasing her mother, Isabel wrests control of her personal life from her father and makes her rite of passage into adulthood.

Among the novel's large cast of secondary characters, Raymond da Costa is clearly the most important, for he shares the stage with Isabel for much of her life—just as he has planned it. Desperate to erase his own failure to earn a doctorate in physics, Ray becomes obsessed with the desire to father a genius. He is profoundly disappointed when first-born Peter is, despite all Ray's best efforts, nothing more than a perfectly normal boy, so when Isabel proves to be gifted, Ray will brook no interference with his plans for her. Although he claims that everything he does for Isabel is intended to promote her best interests, that is clearly not the case. He bullies his wife into relinquishing any authority over her beloved daughter, and he selfishly isolates Isabel from family and friends, making her utterly dependent on him. Like the sinister hypnotist Svengali in George du Maurier's 1894 novel *Trilby*, Ray intends to persuade his daughter to do his bidding, and he will share in her success. In effect, Ray intends to live through Isabel, and he nearly succeeds.

None of the novel's other secondary characters is as fully realized as Raymond. In fact, they tend to function as plot devices, helping to move forward the novel's parallel narratives, and foils, underscoring by their contrasting characteristics the distinctive qualities of *Prizes'* three scientists. Several are also important to the novel's thematic issues.

THEMATIC DEVELOPMENT

Segal's exploration of the personal and professional lives of his three scientists dramatizes one of the novel's major themes—the high cost of success. While all experience the exhilaration of scientific discovery, the "unadulterated joy" of which the narrator speaks in the final chapter (447), they are on more intimate terms with disappointment and betrayal, sacrifice and pain. Like the central characters of *Doctors*, they may be engaged in activities that have the potential to eliminate human suffering, but their efforts do not give them immunity from the ravages of time, the vagaries of fate, and the consequences of human weakness.

Although Adam, for instance, is a committed father, a compassionate physician, and a generous researcher, he cannot keep himself from loving Anya and thereby betraying his marriage. With Anya, he knows the real joy of spiritual and intellectual companionship, so he purchases her love at the cost of his family, especially his daughter, and his own self-respect. In the ensuing years, Adam successfully reclaims his daughter and his honor as well as unlocking some of the secrets of the body's immune system, but his own science is unable to cure the disease that eventually erases the intellect and ravages the body of a man at the height of his powers. Against Alzheimer's disease, Adam can do nothing but orchestrate his own death. A Nobel Prize does not bring with it the gift of life.

For Isabel, the price of success is her childhood. While her brother Peter is fretting about his possible selection to the soccer team and his date for the senior prom, Isabel is fending off attacks on her master's thesis and earning international acclaim. Driven by her father to achieve her potential as well as by her own relentless intelligence and desire to please, Isabel regretfully acknowledges in the pages of her journal that her life has been a list of nevers. She has never gone to summer camp, never traveled, never played tennis (until Jerry Pracht enters her life), never had a friend. That Isabel is as normal and well adjusted as she is has everything to do with her own inner resources and nothing whatsoever to do with the adults who should have ensured that her genius was not allowed to be more important than her whole self.

Segal hammers home his point about the cost of Isabel's genius with the secondary character of Jerry Pracht. The handsome son of her thesis advisor, Jerry hides his intelligence behind a comic disdain for anything serious. Rather than pursue his interest in astronomy, he opts instead for the world of professional tennis, determined to escape "the monkey house of genius" (149) and the fate of his schoolmate, Darius Miller. Jerry, as he confides in Isabel, and Darius had been friends at a school for gifted children. The Millers, however, who had no tolerance for activities that "wasted the time" of their son, had abruptly ended their relationship when Darius broke his arm as Jerry was teaching him to roller-skate. Shortly thereafter and just weeks before his fifteenth birthday, Darius had committed suicide, unable to "bear the thought of growing old" (176). In response, a devastated Jerry had dropped out of school, determined not to "serve the system that had crushed Darrie" (177).

Jerry confides his story to provide Isabel with a context for his life choices. He does not want her to believe that he is a "senseless weirdo" (177). Yet the tale, as Isabel is aware, has the potential to become her own, just as it could have been Jerry's had his parents insisted that he live out their expectations for him. Because they give him the freedom, however, to become himself in his own way and at his own pace, Jerry eventually matures into his intellect, abandoning the tennis court for the laboratory—and a life with Isabel. Taken together, then, the example of Jerry Pracht, the cautionary tale of Darius Miller, and the experience of Isabel da Costa serve as a powerful indictment of the perversion of young genius.

If the lives of Segal's three scientists are any indication, the price of success may be far too high. Granted, the quest for a Nobel Prize-winning discovery can result in significant contributions to humanity's future, but it can also compromise the very humanity of those who strive for it. Gregory Morgenstern, for instance, betrays his son-in-law, Sandy Raven, to achieve the ultimate reward, and Dmitri Avilov, in addition to abandoning his wife because she is unable to bear children, compromises his ethics by performing experimental surgery on desperate patients from the haven of a Caribbean island. Moreover, winning the prize guarantees neither happiness nor contentment. In fact, it promises nothing but an ephemeral pleasure, for it can have as little substance as Hollywood fame. As the epigraph to the novel's final chapter suggests, the human spirit causes our relentless striving "after knowledge infinite," and it will give us no peace until we attain "the sweet fruition of an earthly crown." It is, however, only an "earthly crown," as transitory as human existence, its brilliance doomed to tarnish. Of far more significance, Segal makes clear in the novel's final paragraphs, are love and human relationships. The person who sacrifices them is truly impoverished.

In those final paragraphs, Segal focuses on the winners' responses to their prize. It is sufficient to none. The day after the ceremony, for instance, Dmitri Avilov is "already hungry again" (468). Possessing the Nobel Prize has satisfied only temporarily his need for honors. In contrast, Anya Coopersmith, who has accepted the award for her deceased husband, takes pleasure in "the gentle flutterings of new life within" (468). The "miracle" child that she will bear connects her to something real, something meaningful, something that will outlast the glory of the moment. For Isabel da Costa, those same rewards are promised in her relationship with Jerry. In fact, theirs is, the narrator observes, "the ultimate prize" (468). Clearly, nothing else is worth the price of self, and that is the other major theme of *Prizes*.

A FEMINIST READING OF *PRIZES*

The relationship between Isabel and her father (indeed all of the father-daughter relationships in the novel) provides the feminist critic with an important analytical focus. In fact, it reveals much about the power of men to shape the lives of the women who love them. The feminist critic, as explained in chapter 4, examines literature through the lens of gender differences and gender expectations to reveal the degree to which they define women's lives and experiences. As the first man in his daughter's life, the father exerts tremendous power, shaping her attitudes about both herself and other men. Because he is, as Lynda E. Boose notes, the "chief authorizing figure and primary model for the daughter's later male relationships," his treatment of her has a significant effect on her "relationship to the world beyond her father's house" (38). Given this perspective, the father-daughter relationships in *Prizes* lend a provocative subtext to Segal's primary focus.

The da Costa father-daughter relationship, the most important in the novel, is particularly chilling because Raymond justifies his actions as being in Isabel's best interests when in fact his own needs clearly guide his decisions. To overcome his own sense of failure, inferiority, and insignificance, Raymond assumes control of Isabel's life. In what amounts to a kind of intellectual incest, her achievements are his achievements, for, "after all," Ray thinks, "when they trumpeted Isabel's genius, were they not also implicitly praising him?" (91). Thus Ray lives in dread of the day that Isabel surpasses him in intelligence and no longer needs his guidance (131). To delay that inevitability and to protect his position when it happens, he has made Isabel utterly dependent on him, cutting her off from her mother and brother and isolating her in a "cloistered life" (234).

For most of her life, Isabel is content with her relationship with her father because he nurtures her intellectual growth. Certainly, she feels the lack of her mother's and brother's presence. Yet she has come to depend on Ray's affirmation and fears its loss. When other teens her age are rebelling against parental authority, Isabel, much to her mother's regret (117), submits to her father's decisions, seldom expressing her own preferences (except in her journal). She has, by her own admission, "lived with him and for him" (403) for too much of her life ever to think of disappointing him. Were Isabel a lesser person, the effect of Ray's domination might destroy her happiness, but it clearly stunts her emotional development. In fact, it makes her a potential Toni Coopersmith or Judy Morgenstern, daughters so enamored of their fathers that they cannot find comparable husbands.

From the time that Adam Coopersmith meets Antonia Hartwell, he doubts his ability to win her from her father, a powerful political kingmaker known as "The Boss." Thomas Hartwell's two sons may lack his competitive drive and fierce ambition, but Toni, his beloved "Skipper," has enough to spare. She relishes life in her father's world and is clearly his "favorite son" (63). From Adam's perspective, however, Toni's relationship with her father is debilitating because it prevents her from establishing strong emotional bonds with another man. When they meet, for instance, she is having an affair with the attorney general, a married man who is nearly her father's age and who wields nearly the same sort of power and is thus his substitute.

Although Toni eventually marries Adam and relocates to Boston to be with him, he never entirely succeeds in "[tearing her] away from her father's smothering sphere of influence" (77). Their frequent telephone conversations are important to her emotional equilibrium because he, not Adam, is her chief confidant, and his world of power and influence is far more attractive to her than Adam's sterile laboratory. To the novel's end, Thomas Hartwell is "The Boss" in his daughter's life, so to some extent, the Coopersmith divorce is inevitable. Adam could never replace an adored and adoring father.

Surprisingly perhaps, given his understanding of the Hartwell father-daughter relationship, Adam establishes a similar relationship with his own daughter, Heather, becoming her trusted confidant and primary source of self-affirmation (84), and so it is with Gregory and Judy Morgenstern. In Sandy Raven, she marries the man most like her father and most likely to please her father. When he turns out to be merely Sandy Raven, however, Judy retreats quickly to the paternal embrace. Even Jerry Pracht, for all his quirky normality and genuine love of Isabel, is a bit like the father he replaces in her life in his desire to care for and protect her. Virtually all of the father-daughter relationships in *Prizes* stunt the emotional development of the daughters, making them dependent, submissive, and eager to please. Virtually all of them help to create the kind of women traditionally desired in a patriarchal, or male dominated, society.

Such women, as we see them in the novel, are utterly powerless and easily abused. Anya Avilova, for instance, a Russian émigré who lacks the credentials to support herself properly, is abandoned by her husband when he learns conclusively that she will never be able to bear his child. Similarly, Muriel da Costa, against her own convictions about Isabel's best interests, submits to Raymond's rule rather than "allow her [daughter] to be to be [sic] the mutilated prize in a parental tug-of-war" (68). Others, such as Judy and Toni, are virtually ignored by their husbands, who pursue their important work as if nothing else matters. Even professional women such as Lisl Rudolph, Adam's substitute mother and an accomplished psychologist, and Anya Avilova Coopersmith, a superb clinician, play subordinate roles to their loving husbands' careers. Such evidence makes readers wonder whether Isabel would be quite so successful if she were an intellectually assertive woman and not a precocious girl who thus poses little threat to the largely male scientific community.

The role of motherhood in *Prizes* also provides an interesting perspective on the status of women in a patriarchal society. Basically, the novel depicts women who abdicate their responsibility to motherhood, or who choose not to mother at all, as monsters. In the first category is Toni Coopersmith, who prefers her career to her daughter, placing Heather in the care of a nanny and even sending her to boarding school when neglect and unhappiness drive her to rebellion. Sandy Raven's mother, who abandons her young son almost as soon as he is born, is also in this category. In the second category is Kim Tower, the Hollywood starlet-turned-producer who cares for nobody but herself. Segal's depiction of these women is so unsympathetic that readers might easily overlook Adam's role in Toni's failure as a mother or the Hollywood system's own use and abuse of Kim (no matter how willing she might be to submit to it).

In contrast, the women accorded positive treatment in the novel are those who desire motherhood and struggle for it, such as Lisl Rudolph and Anya Coopersmith, however unsuccessful their quest may be. Even Muriel da Costa, who seemingly abdicates motherhood (and who has also committed adultery), earns readers' sympathies because she submits to Ray's authority to save Isabel. In other words, she does what every mother "should" do—sacrifice herself for her child.

For women, the world of *Prizes* is undeniably patriarchal, for its boundaries are circumscribed not only by the men who shape their sense of self but also by the roles they are expected to play. However benevolent their motives and actions, fathers help to shape the kind of women who traditionally inhabit such a world, women who are submissive and supportive and who idealize the men in their lives. Motherhood is the highest role they can assume in this world. A feminist reading of *Prizes*, then, extends the novel's primary focus: Not only is the cost of success high, but so, too, is the cost of womanhood.

Bibliography

Note: All page numbers in the text refer to the paperback editions of Erich Segal's novels, with the exception of *Love Story* and *Prizes*. Page references to these books are to the hardcover editions.

WORKS BY ERICH SEGAL

Fiction

Acts of Faith. New York: Bantam, 1992; Bantam, 1993.
The Class. New York: Bantam, 1985; Bantam, 1986.
Doctors. New York: Bantam, 1988; Bantam, 1989.
Fairy Tale. New York: Harper & Row, 1973.
Love Story. New York: Harper & Row, 1970.
Man, Woman and Child. New York: Harper & Row, 1980; Bantam, 1993.
Oliver's Story. New York: Harper & Row, 1977; Avon, 1978.
Prizes. New York: Ballantine, 1995.

Essays

"Heavy Breathing in Arcadia." *New York Times Book Review*, 29 September 1985: 1, 48–49.

"The Limits of Sport." *The New Republic*, 16 September 1981: 17–19.
"Slouching Towards America." *The New Republic*, 2 October 1976: 25–27.

Scholarly Works

Caesar Augustus: Seven Aspects. Ed. Erich Segal and Fergus Millar. Oxford: Oxford University Press, 1984.
The Dialogues of Plato. Ed. Erich Segal. New York: Bantam, 1986.
Euripides: A Collection of Critical Essays. Ed. Erich Segal. Englewood Cliffs, N.J.: Prentice-Hall, 1968.
The Oxford Readings in Greek Tragedy. Ed. Erich Segal. New York: Harper & Row, 1983; Oxford: Oxford University Press, 1983.
Plautus: Three Comedies. Edited and translated by Erich Segal. New York: Harper & Row, 1969.
Roman Laughter: The Comedy of Plautus. Cambridge, Mass.: Harvard University Press, 1968; revised and enlarged, London: Oxford University Press, 1987.

Screenplays

A Change of Seasons. Ransohoff-Columbia, 1980.
The Games. 20th Century-Fox, 1969.
Jennifer on My Mind. United Artists, 1971.
Love Story. Paramount Pictures, 1970.
Man, Woman and Child. Paramount Pictures, 1983.
Oliver's Story. Paramount Pictures, 1978.
R.P.M. Stanley Kramer-Columbia Pictures, 1970.
Yellow Submarine. By Erich Segal, Lee Minoff, Al Brodax, and Jack Mendelsohn. United Artists, 1968.

WORKS ABOUT ERICH SEGAL

Arnold, Gary. "One Big Sappy Family." *Washington Post*, 4 April 1983: B2.
Bannon, Barbara A. "Authors and Editors." *Publisher's Weekly*, 2 February 1970: 51–53.
Casey, Phil. "Erich Segal: The Loved One—Poor Little Kitsch Boy." *Washington Post*, 11 February 1971: C1, 3.
Chambers, Andrea. "*Love Story*'s Erich Segal Writes a New Best-Selling Novel With a Touch of Class." *People Weekly*, 13 May 1985: 113–14, 119.

Darrach, Brad. "Being Erich Means Always Having to Say You're Sorry." *Life*, 4 June 1971: 77.

Dye, Mary S. "Erich Segal." *Dictionary of Literary Biography Yearbook 1986*: 323–28.

Ephron, Nora. "Mush." *Esquire*, June 1971: 91–92, 152, 154, 156–57.

"Erich Segal." *Contemporary Authors*. Vol. 25–28: 645–46.

"Erich Segal." *Current Biography 1971*: 387–89.

"Erich Segal's Identity Crisis." Ed. Paul Goldberger. *New York Times Magazine*, 13 June 1971: 16–17, 24, 36, 40, 45.

Hutchens, John K. "One Thing and Another." *Saturday Review*, 14 February 1970: 35.

Johnston, Laurie, and Albin Krebs. "Erich Segal Returns Home, to Yale." *New York Times*, 4 September 1981: C18.

Kael, Pauline. "Epic and Crumbcrusher." *New Yorker*, 26 December 1970: 50–54.

Kanfer, Stefan. "The Love Bug." *Time*, 21 December 1970: 55–56.

Keerdoja, Eileen, et al. "Segal: Another Novel About Love." *Newsweek*, 5 May 1980: 16.

Kronenberger, J., Ed. "Is the Family Obsolete?" *Look*, 26 January 1971: 35–36.

Martin, Judith. "A Best-Selling Novelist and Successful Son." *Washington Post*, 11 February 1970: B1, 3.

Mercier, J. Y. "Erich Segal's Last Last Interview." *Vogue*, August 1971: 89+.

Minoff, Lee. " 'Yellow Submarine' Passenger List." *New York Times Magazine*, 4 July 1971: 3.

Raymont, Henry. "Book Unit Rejects 'Love Story.' " *New York Times*, 22 January 1971: A16.

———. "Judges of Book Awards Revolt on Use of Nationwide Polling." *New York Times*, 26 January 1971: A22.

"Segal the Scholar." *Time*, 15 March 1971: 52–53.

Smith, Wendy. "Segal: 'Class' Author Comes Down to Earth." *Chicago Tribune*, 5 May 1985: 41, 45.

Wilkes, P. "Yale is No. 1 with the Promoter and the Idol." *Look*, 6 April 1971: 60–62.

REVIEWS AND CRITICISM

Love Story

America, July 1970: 715.

Black, Campbell. Review of *Love Story*. *New Statesman*, 28 August 1970: 249.

"Coming in from the Cold." *Christian Science Monitor*, 30 April 1970: 13.

Gardner, Richard M. "Stereotypes and Sentimentality: The Coarser Sieve." *Midwest Quarterly* 29 (1988): 232–48.

"Grim Weeper." *Times Literary Supplement*, 4 September 1970: 965.

Lehmann-Haupt, Christopher. "Private Screenings." *New York Times*, 13 February 1970: K35.

Levin, Martin. "Reader's Report." *New York Times Book Review*, 8 March 1970: 31.

New Yorker, 28 February 1970: 116.

New Yorker, 24 October 1970: 170.

Oberbeck, S. K. "Clean Book." *Newsweek*, 9 March 1970: 94–95.

Observer (London), 23 April 1970: 23.

Observer (London), 10 January 1971: 23.

Park, Clara Claiborne. "As We Like It: How a Girl Can Be Smart and Still Popular." In *The Woman's Part: Feminist Criticism of Shakespeare*. Eds. Carolyn Ruth Swift Lenz, Gayle Green, and Carol Thomas Neely. Urbana and Chicago: University of Illinois Press, 1983: 100–116.

Publisher's Weekly, 1 December 1969: 39.

Publisher's Weekly, 19 October 1970: 55.

Saal, Rollene W. "Pick of the Paperbacks." *Saturday Review*, 26 December 1970: 30.

Spectator, 29 August 1970: 217.

Spilka, Mark. "Erich Segal as Little Nell, or The Real Meaning of *Love Story*." *Journal of Popular Culture* (1972): 782–98.

Weeks, Edward. Review of *Love Story*. *Atlantic Monthly*, June 1970: 124–25.

Fairy Tale

Adams, Phoebe. Review of *Fairy Tale*. *Atlantic Monthly*, April 1973: 128.

Clemons, Walter. "Hollow Hilarity." *Newsweek*, 9 April 1973: 114.

Lee, Susan Previant, and Leonard Ross. Review of *Fairy Tale*. *New Times Book Review*, 25 March 1973: 46.

New Yorker, 7 April 1973: 151.

Oliver's Story

Brookner, Anita. "What Marcie Knew." *Times Literary Supplement*, 13 May 1977: 581.

Clarke, Gerald. "Woe Revisited." *Time*, 21 March 1977: 93.

Lehmann-Haupt, Christopher. "Books of The Times." *New York Times*, 25 February 1977: C21.

Lingeman, Richard R. "The Son of 'Love Story'." *New York Times Book Review*, 6 March 1977: 6–7.

New Yorker, 18 April 1977: 157.

Observer (London), 5 June 1977: 29.

Publisher's Weekly, 24 January 1977: 327.

Publisher's Weekly, 9 January 1978: 80.

Sinclair, Dorothy. Review of *Oliver's Story*. *West Coast Review of Books*, May 1977:
    30.
Village Voice, 29 March 1977: 44.
Wall Street Journal, 25 July 1977: 10.

Man, Woman and Child

Johnson, Priscilla. Review of *Man, Woman and Child*. *School Library Journal*, Oc-
    tober 1980: 168.
Levin, Martin. "Laughs and Tears." *New York Times Book Review*, 8 June 1980: 14,
    41.
Publisher's Weekly, 28 March 1980: 43.
Publisher's Weekly, 24 April 1981: 74.
Sheppard, R. Z. "Togetherness." *Time*, 26 May 1980: 92.
Smothers, Joyce. Review of *Man, Woman and Child*. *Library Journal*, 15 April 1980:
    1005.

The Class

Isaacs, Susan. "The Yard and the World." *New York Times Book Review*, 21 April
    1985: 9.
Leber, Michele. Review of *The Class*. *Library Journal*, 15 April 1985: 87.
Los Angeles Times Book Review, 19 May 1985: 3.
Publisher's Weekly, 15 March 1985: 103.
Shapiro, Laura. "Halcyon Harvard." *Newsweek*, 13 May 1985: 83.
Sheppard, R. Z. "Yardbirds." *Time*, 13 May 1985: 80–81.
Wall Street Journal, 22 April 1985: 26.
West Coast Review of Books, July 1985: 26.

Doctors

Observer (London), 19 February 1989: 44.
Publisher's Weekly, 15 July 1988: 56.
Reed, Kit. Review of *Doctors*. *New Times Book Review*, 18 September 1988: 32.
West Coast Review of Books, July 1988: 31.

Acts of Faith

"Ads for Bantam Bestseller Rejected by Catholic Papers." *Publisher's Weekly*, 13
    April 1992: 12.

Blank, Denise. Review of *Acts of Faith*. *Booklist*, 1 February 1992: 986.
Burgess, Anthony. "Orthodox Intentions." *Times Literary Supplement*, 14 February 1992: 23.
Kaufman, Joanne. Review of *Acts of Faith*. *People Weekly*, 8 June 1992: 29.
Ottenhoff, John. "Fast Food for the Journey." *The Christian Century*, 12–19 August 1992: 747–49.
Steinberg, Sybil. Review of *Acts of Faith*. *Publisher's Weekly*, 27 January 1992: 86.

Prizes

Chamberlain, Erna. Review of *Prizes*. *Library Journal*, 15 February 1995: 183.
Korn, Eric. "Going for the Gongs." *Times Literary Supplement*, 9 June 1995: 29.
Los Angeles Times Book Review, 5 March 1995: 10.
Seaman, Donna. Review of *Prizes*. *Booklist*, 1 January 1995: 91.
Steinberg, Sybil. Review of *Prizes*. *Publisher's Weekly*, 2 January 1995: 57.

OTHER SECONDARY SOURCES

Appignanesi, Richard, and Chris Garratt. *Introducing Postmodernism*. New York: Totem Books, 1995.
Berger, Arthur Asa. *Cultural Criticism*: *A Primer of Key Concepts*. Foundations of Popular Culture, Vol. 4. Thousand Oaks, Calif.: Sage Publications, 1995.
Boose, Lynda E. "The Father's House and the Daughter in It: The Structures of Western Culture's Daughter-Father Relationship." In *Daughters and Fathers*. Ed. Lynda E. Boose and Betty S. Flowers. Baltimore: Johns Hopkins University Press, 1989: 19–74.
Braudy, Leo. "The Form of the Sentimental Novel." *Novel 7* (1973): 5–13.
Gelderman, Carol. *Mary McCarthy. A Life*. New York: St. Martin's Press, 1988.
Kaplan, Fred. *Sacred Tears. Sentimentality in Victorian Literature*. Princeton, N.J.: Princeton University Press, 1987.
Richter, David H., ed. *The Critical Tradition. Classic Texts and Contemporary Trends*. New York: St. Martin's Press, 1989.
Showalter, Elaine. "The Feminist Critical Revolution." In *The New Feminist Criticism: Essays on Women, Literature, and Theory*. Ed. Elaine Showalter. London: Virago Press, 1986: 3–17.
———. "Toward a Feminist Poetics." In *The New Feminist Criticism: Essays on Women, Literature, and Theory*. Ed. Elaine Showalter. London: Virago Press, 1986: 125–43.
Swales, Martin. *The German* Bildungsroman *from* Wieland *to* Hesse. Princeton, N.J.: Princeton University Press, 1978.

Index

ABC (American Broadcasting Corporation), 6

Academy Awards, 7

Ackerman, Bernie (*Man, Woman and Child*), 48–49, 55–56

Ackerman, David (*Man, Woman and Child*), 49, 56

Acts of Faith, 11, 15–16, 17; 93–108; characterization, 98–103; controversy about, 104; cultural critique of, 106–8; narrative strategies, 96–98; plot development, 94–96; significance of names, 102–3; themes, 103–6

Adams, Alice, 63

The American (James), comparison to, 52

Anderson, Grete (*Doctors*), 82–83, 87

Anderson, Robert, 37

Anderson, Tod (*The Class*), 74

Ariel (*Acts of Faith*), 102, 104

Avilov, Dmitri (*Prizes*), 117–18

Balzac, Honore de, 15

Barrett, Bozo (*Love Story*), 26–27, 29

Barrett, Mrs. Oliver, III (*Love Story*), 29

Barrett, Oliver, III (*Love Story* and *Oliver's Story*), 24–30, 37–39

Barrett, Oliver, IV (*Love Story* and *Oliver's Story*), 12, 14–16, 19, 21–39, 41–43, 45, 60

The Beatles, 4, 5

Beckwith, Jessica (*Man, Woman and Child*), 49–51, 53, 56

Beckwith, Paula (*Man, Woman and Child*), 49–51, 53, 57

Beckwith, Robert (*Man, Woman and Child*), 15–16, 45–53, 55, 56, 57

Beckwith, Sheila Goodhart (*Man, Woman and Child*), 16, 45, 47–48, 50–57

Beller, Professor Aaron (*Acts of Faith*), 95, 99, 103–4

Bellow, Saul, 5

Ben-Ami, Boaz (*Acts of Faith*), 103

Ben-Ami, Elisha (*Acts of Faith*), 95, 101, 108

Bennett, Colonel Abraham Lincoln (*Doctors*), 81, 87

''Bereft'' (Frost), 62–63

Bildungsroman, 63, 68, 78, 84. *See also* Genres, literary

"The Boss" (*Prizes*), 14, 119–20
Boston Marathon, 1, 2
Boswell, James, comparison to, 66
Bunyan, John, 94
"Burnt Norton" (Eliot), 67

Casey, Ben, comparison to, 86
Castellano, Isobel (*Doctors*), 79, 83
Castellano, Laura (*Doctors*), 13, 78–80, 83–84, 86–87, 88, 91
Castellano, Luis (*Doctors*), 79–80, 83
Cavilleri, Jennifer (*Love Story* and *Oliver's Story*), 11–12, 14–15, 19–32, 34–39, 41, 43
Cavilleri, Phil (*Love Story* and *Oliver's Story*), 23, 25, 27, 33–34, 36, 38, 42–43
Chaplin, Bill (*Doctors*), 85–86
Characters. *See individual characters*
Chariton of Aphrodisias, 9
Cinematic style, 12, 22, 46, 65, 110–11
The Class, 7, 12, 14, 15–17, 58–75, 78, 98; characterization, 60–63, 66–67; cinematic style, 65; epigraphs, 60–63, 67–68; generic conventions, 63–64; Marxist analysis of, 71–74; narrative strategies, 64–68; themes, 68–71
Class Reunion (Jaffe), comparison to, 63–64
"College" novel, 63–64. *See also* Genres, literary
The Confessions of St. Augustine, 97
Confidant figure, 36, 48
Coopersmith, Adam (*Prizes*), 11, 14, 109–13, 116, 119–21
Coopersmith, Antonia (Toni) Hartwell (*Prizes*), 113, 119–21
Coopersmith, Anya Avilova (*Prizes*), 11, 110, 113, 116–18, 120–21
Coopersmith, Heather (*Prizes*), 113, 116, 120–21
Cultural literary criticism, 54–55. *See also* Theory, literary
cummings, e. e., 61

da Costa, Isabel (*Prizes*), 110–12, 114–20
da Costa, Muriel (*Prizes*), 115, 119–21
da Costa, Peter (*Prizes*), 115–16, 119
da Costa, Raymond (*Prizes*), 110, 112, 114–16, 118–20
Dailey, Janet, 9
Daisy Miller (James), comparison to, 52
Deconstructionist literary criticism, 88–90. *See also* Theory, literary
Dickens, Charles, 10
Doctors, 11–13, 15–16, 77–91, 96, 116; characterization, 78–83; deconstructionist interpretation of, 88–91; epigraphs, 77, 84–85; narrative strategies, 83–85; themes, 85–88
Dr. Faustus (Marlowe), comparison to, 95, 99
du Maurier, George, 116
Dwyer, Cheryl (*Doctors*), 84
Dwyer, Hank (*Doctors*), 82–84, 87

Eli (*Acts of Faith*), 95, 101, 108
Eliot, Andrew (*The Class*), 60, 65–67, 69, 71, 73
Eliot, Lizzie (*The Class*), 74
Eliot, T. S., 60, 67–68
Emerson, Ralph Waldo, 61–62
Epigraphs, use of, 37, 51–52, 60–63, 67–68, 77, 84–85, 96–97, 118

Fairy Tale, 6–7
Feminist literary criticism, 39–41, 118–19. *See also* Theory, literary
Fitzgerald, Francis Scott, 52
Four Quartets (Eliot), 67
Francis, James (*Oliver's Story*), 39
Freudianism, 29. *See also* Oedipus complex; Theory, literary
Frost, Robert, 62–63

The Games, 5
Genres, literary: *Bildungsroman*, 63, 68, 78, 84; "college" novel, 63–64; novel of manners, 55; romance novel, 9,

20–22, 25; sentimental novel, 9–16,
  20–22
Gilbert, Jason (*The Class*), 14, 61–62,
  64–65, 68–69, 74
Goethe, Johann Wolfgang von, 63
Golden Globe Awards, 7
Goldman, Steve and Esther (*Acts of
  Faith*), 103
Gordon, Mary, 108
The Group (McCarthy), comparison to,
  63
Guérin, Jean-Claude (*Man, Woman and
  Child*), 15, 46–51, 53–54, 56–57
Guérin, Nicole (*Man, Woman and
  Child*), 46–47, 51–52, 56–57

Hardt, Ernesto (*Acts of Faith*), 98, 103,
  105, 107
Harrison, P. Herbert (*Man, Woman
  and Child*), 52, 56
Hartwell, Thomas (*Prizes*), 14, 119–20
Hartwell, Toni, 113, 119–21
Harvard University, 3, 16, 59–61, 67,
  73–74
Hawthorne, Nathaniel, 52
"Heavy Breathing in Arcadia," 9
Hemingway, Ernest, 52
Hogan, Timothy (*Acts of Faith*), 94–98,
  100–108
Holmes, Oliver Wendell, 85
Holocaust, 81, 83, 86–87
Hsiang, Dr. (*Doctors*), 88

I Never Sang for My Father (Anderson), 37

Jack and the Beanstalk, use of tale, 7
Jaffe, Marshall (*Doctors*), 79, 87
Jaffe, Rona, 63–64
James, Henry, 52
James, William, 67
Jennifer on My Mind, 5
Johnson, Samuel, 66
Judaism, 104–8

Keller, Cathy (*The Class*), 71
Keller, George (*The Class*), 17, 60, 62–
  66, 70–71

Kildare, Dr., comparison to, 86
King Lear (Shakespeare), comparison
  to, 94–95
Kolozsdi, Gyuri. *See* Keller, George

Lambros, Sara (*The Class*), 70, 74
Lambros, Ted (*The Class*), 16, 60–61,
  64–66, 69–70, 73–74
Landsmann, Bennett (*Doctors*), 80–83,
  86–87, 91
Landsmann, Hannah (*Doctors*), 81, 87
Landsmann, Herschel (*Doctors*), 81
The Last Convertible (Myrer), compari-
  son to, 64
The Late George Apley (Marquand),
  comparison to, 21
Lazarus, Howie (*Doctors*), 82, 86
Lazarus, Seth (*Doctors*), 82, 86, 91
"The Limits of Sport," 1
"Little Gidding" (Eliot), 68
Livingston, Barney (*Doctors*), 14, 78–
  80, 84–86, 88, 90–91
Livingston, Harold (*Doctors*), 80, 86–
  87, 91
Livingston, Harry (*Doctors*), 84, 88
London, Dr. (*Oliver's Story*), 34, 36–38,
  42
"The Love-Song of J. Alfred Pru-
  frock" (Eliot), 60
Love Story, 2–6, 8–12, 14–15, 19–32, 34,
  36–39, 45–46, 59–60; characteriza-
  tion, 22–24; cinematic style, 22; film
  version, 4, 6–7, 20; generic conven-
  tions, 20–22, 25; psychological analysis of, 29–30; publishing history,
  19–20; themes, 25–30
Luria, Daniel (*Acts of Faith*), 17, 93–
  104, 106–108
Luria, Deborah (*Acts of Faith*), 93–108
Luria, Rav Moses (*Acts of Faith*), 93,
  94, 98–103
Luria, Rena (*Acts of Faith*), 99
Lurie, Dan. *See* Luria, Daniel

Mailer, Norman, 7
Malamud, Bernard, 108
Man, Woman and Child, 7, 14–16; 45–

58; characterization, 48–51; cinematic style, 46; cultural critique of, 54–57; epigraph, 51–52; film version, 7; narrative strategies, 46–48; themes, 45, 51–54
The Marble Faun, 52
Marlowe, Christopher, 95, 99
Marquand, John P., 21
Marxist literary criticism, 54–55, 71–73. *See also* Theory, literary
McCarthy, Mary, 63
McGraw, Ali, 4, 20
Mephistopheles, comparison to, 95, 99
Miller, Darius (*Prizes*), 117
Morgenstern, Gregory (*Prizes*), 113–14, 117, 120
Mortimer, Lance (*Doctors*), 82–83, 86–87
Mr. Sammler's Planet (Bellow), 5
Myrer, Anton, 64

Narrative strategies, 20–22, 34–36, 46–48, 64–68, 83–85, 96–98, 110–12
Nash, Marcie Binnendale (*Oliver's Story*), 16, 32–39, 41–43
National Book Award, 5
Newall, Dickie (*The Class*), 73, 74
Nobel Prize, 11, 14, 16, 109–111, 117
Novel of manners, 55. *See also* Genres, literary

Oedipus complex, 29, 38–39
Oliver's Story, 6, 14–15, 31–43, 45; characterization, 32–33; confidant figure, 36; feminist analysis of, 39–43; film version, 7; narrative strategies, 34–36; themes, 37–39
Olympic Games, 6
O'Neal, Ryan, 4

Peace Corps, 6, 26
The Pilgrim's Progress (Bunyan), comparison to, 94
Portnoy's Complaint (Roth), 10
The Portrait of a Lady (James), comparison to, 52

Pracht, Jerry (*Prizes*), 115, 117, 118, 120
Prizes, 7, 11, 14–17, 109–21; characterization, 112–16; cinematic style, 110–11; epigraph, 118; feminist analysis of, 118–21; narrative strategies, 110–12; themes, 116–18
Protestantism, 106–8
Psychological literary criticism, 29. *See also* Oedipus complex; Theory, literary

Raposo, Joe, 3, 4
Raven, Judy Morgenstern (*Prizes*), 113–14, 119–20
Raven, Sandy (*Prizes*), 17, 109–14, 117, 120–21
Raven, Sidney (*Prizes*), 113–14
Rodgers, Richard, 4
Rogers, Rosemary, 9
Roman Catholicism, 16, 84, 104–8
Romance novel, 9, 20–22, 25. *See also* Genres, literary
Romeo and Juliet (Shakespeare), comparison to, 95
Rossi, Daniel (*The Class*), 17, 62, 65–66, 70
Rossi, Maria (*The Class*), 70
Roth, Philip, 10
R.P.M., 5
Rudolph, Lisl (*Prizes*), 113, 120–21
Rudolph, Max (*Prizes*), 113

Segal, Erich: academic career, 3, 5–6; awards, 2–3, 5, 7; education, 2–3; Harvard experience, 59–60; marriage, 7; screenwriting, 4, 7, 12, 20; sportscasting, 6; writing career, 2, 4–8, 14–17; youth, 2. *See also specific titles*
Sentimental novel, 9–16, 20–22. *See also* Genres, literary
Shakespeare, William, 94–95
Simpson, Stephen (*Oliver's Story*), 33–34
Singer, Isaac Bashevis, 108
"Slouching Towards America," 7–8

Stein, Joanna (*Oliver's Story*), 33–34, 42

Stereotypes, use of, 12–14, 21, 23, 82–83, 95

Styron, William, 5

Superior Women (Adams), comparison to, 63

Svengali, comparison to, 116

Talbot, Palmer (*Doctors*), 79

Tatius, Achilles, 9

Taubman, Rochelle, 114, 121

Themes, 16–17, 25–28, 37–39, 51–54, 68–71, 85–88, 103–6, 116–18

Theory, literary: cultural criticism, 54–55; deconstructionism, 88–90; feminist, 39–41, 118–19; Freudianism, 29; Marxist, 54, 55, 71–73; psychological, 29

Thoreau, Henry David, 61

Tower, Kim (*Prizes*), 114, 121

Trilby (du Maurier), 116

Unified Field Theory, 16, 110

Updike, John, 5, 67

van Nostrand, Margo (*Man, Woman and Child*), 48, 50, 52, 55

Venarguès, Louis (*Man, Woman and Child*), 57

Vidal, Gore, 7

Vidal, Miriam (*Acts of Faith*), 102

Wiesel, Elie, 7

Wigglesworth, Mike (*The Class*), 73

Wilhelm Meister's Apprenticeship (Goethe), 63

Williams, William Carlos, 84

Wilson, Gavin (*Man, Woman and Child*), 50, 53

Wyman, Peter (*Doctors*), 87–88

Yale University, 3–6, 61

Yellow Submarine, 4–5

About the Author

LINDA C. PELZER is Associate Professor of English at Wesley College in Dover, Delaware. A specialist in American literature, she is a former Fulbright scholar. Her study, *Mary Higgins Clark*, was the first volume published in the Critical Companions to Popular Contemporary Writers series. She is currently working on a biography of Martha Gellhorn.

Other Titles in
Critical Companions to Popular Contemporary Writers
Kathleen Gregory Klein, Series Editor

V. C. Andrews: A Critical Companion
E. D. Huntley

Tom Clancy: A Critical Companion
Helen S. Garson

Mary Higgins Clark: A Critical Companion
Linda C. Pelzer

Arthur C. Clarke: A Critical Companion
Robin Anne Reid

James Clavell: A Critical Companion
Gina Macdonald

Pat Conroy: A Critical Companion
Landon C. Burns

Robin Cook: A Critical Companion
Lorena Laura Stookey

Michael Crichton: A Critical Companion
Elizabeth A. Trembley

Howard Fast: A Critical Companion
Andrew Macdonald

Ken Follett: A Critical Companion
Richard C. Turner

John Grisham: A Critical Companion
Mary Beth Pringle

James Herriot: A Critical Companion
Michael J. Rossi

Tony Hillerman: A Critical Companion
John M. Reilly

John Jakes: A Critical Companion
Mary Ellen Jones

Stephen King: A Critical Companion
Sharon A. Russell

Dean Koontz: A Critical Companion
Joan G. Kotker

Anne McCaffrey: A Critical Companion
Robin Roberts

Colleen McCullough: A Critical Companion
Mary Jean DeMarr

James A. Michener: A Critical Companion
Marilyn S. Severson

Anne Rice: A Critical Companion
Jennifer Smith

John Saul: A Critical Companion
Paul Bail

Gore Vidal: A Critical Companion
Susan Baker